Terry Lovell

Consuming Fiction

VERSO

The Imprint of New Left Books

First published by Verso 1987
© Terry Lovell 1987
All rights reserved.

Verso
6 Meard Street, London W1V 3HR
29 West 35th Street, New York, NY 10001 2291

Verso is the imprint of New Left Books

Typeset in Parlament by Leaper & Gard Ltd., Bristol, England.
Printed in Great Britain by the Thetford Press, Norfolk.

British Library Cataloguing in Publication Data

Lovell, Terry
     Consuming fiction.——(Questions for
     feminism).
     1. English fiction——19th century
     History and criticism
     I. Title   II. Series
     823'.009   PR861

ISBN 0-86091-173-X
ISBN 0-86091-885-8 Pbk

Contents

Acknowledgements

This book grew out of a course in the sociology of literature which I taught for a number of years with Simon Frith at Warwick University. My thanks are therefore due first of all to our students who over the years have provided stimulation and encouragement. But above all they are due to Simon, with whom I have exchanged so many ideas that I can no longer claim that they are entirely mine. Convention requires me to add the usual rider absolving him from any responsibility for the bad ideas . . .

My thanks also to all those people who read, and commented on, all or part of earlier drafts, including Bridget Fowler, Gill Frith, Simon Frith, John Goode, Ann Jones, Robin Lenman and Carolyn Steedman. Finally a particularly grateful thank you to Michele Barrett for being such a very helpful editor and for assisting the manuscript through a rather difficult patch.

1.

Introduction: Questions of Marxist Literary Analysis and Questions for Feminism

What place has the novel had, historically, among the 'comp-onents of the national culture' in Britain? What is its relationship, within that culture, to capitalism, to the dominant class of capi-talism and to bourgeois ideology? What part have women played in the production, reproduction and transmission of that culture? These are some of the questions addressed in this work. They arise in relation to a particular tradition of Marxist literary and cultural historiography in Britain, and as such are neither specif-ically nor exclusively questions for feminism. The appearance of this work in a series of that title therefore requires some expla-nation.

The New Left in Britain has developed a rich body of Marxist cultural history and theory. It has traced the contours of a national culture which is the culture of the ruling class, and identified within it a pivotal role played by English literature. Perry Anderson's 1966 essay 'Components of the National Culture' struck the keynote.[1] He characterized the national cul-ture historically, in terms of an absent centre, any viable syn-thesizing sociology. This absence he in turn explained by the relative weakness of Marxism in the intellectual and political for-mation of the labour movement. In continental Europe it was the strength of Marxism which stimulated its most formidable intel-lectual challenge, that mounted by sociological theory, par-ticularly the sociology of Max Weber. Anderson linked this dual absence of Marxism and theoretical sociology from the com-ponents of the national culture to his earlier analysis of the

British ruling class.[2] Historically sweeping, this analysis had located the roots of British capitalism in a Gramscian history of its earlier origins. Britain had been the birthplace of capitalism and its economic and political revolutions were unique. Every subsequent capitalism emerged in the context of a world transformed by this first capitalist formation.

Tom Nairn, taking up and amplifying Anderson's analysis, drew the conclusion that this first capitalism had paid the price of prematurity. It was incomplete.[3] Anderson had argued that the British industrial bourgeoisie had failed to see the revolution through, and had come to terms politically and socially and culturally with the older landed and commercial fractions of capitalism, accepting their leadership of the class as a whole. The more advanced sector of the bourgeoisie who might have been expected to assume command of the class in a new style, and to produce a compelling ideology on which to build its hegemony, was according to Anderson's judgement a sector whose history was one of supine inadequacy, politically and culturally. The best it proved able to produce was utilitarianism, a doctrine unable to inspire a sense of moral unity and purpose in the class whose interests it too manifestly supported, let alone win the hearts and minds of the working class.

Anderson argued that the settling of accounts with the older, largely unreformed fractions of capitalism on terms favourable to them in the early decades of the nineteenth century generated a hybrid ideological synthesis identifiable as a certain intellectual style rather than a clearly defined doctrine. This older, dominant sector of the ruling class consisted in an anachronistic social elite whose roots were in the countryside and the City of London rather than in the new urban centres of the industrial revolution. Its members were amateurs and gentlemen, educated at a small group of public schools and at Oxbridge. Paternalistic in their concept of class, and pragmatic in their thinking, they eschewed 'grand theory' and any attempt at the rational reconstruction of industry or the state. Anderson characterized this ruling elite in terms of a 'pseudo-feudal hierarchy' of rank and ceremony, visible in differences of accent, vocabulary, diet, dress and recreation.

Anderson's companion essay, in which he looked more directly at 'high culture' and scholarship in contemporary Britain, drew attention to the close links between the British literary intelligentsia and the still surviving anachronistic ruling elite: 'An intricate net of kinship linked the traditional lineages which produced scholars and thinkers to each other and to their common social group. The same names occur again and again: Macauley, Trevelyan, Arnold, Vaughan, Strachey, Darwin, Huxley, Stephen, Wedgewood, Hodgkin, and others . . . . Intellectuals were related by family to their class, not by profession to their estate.'[4]

In the nineteenth century this political and intellectual elite were public school and Oxbridge men whose education would have centred on the study of the classics. In the mid-twentieth century, the same names still recur, with the addition of those of a generation of Eastern European white emigrés. But the ideological cement provided by a classical education has been replaced by a broader reformed curriculum and the study of English literature. English literary criticism, Anderson claimed, came to occupy the place left absent at the heart of bourgeois culture by a weak sociological tradition. 'Suppressed and denied in every other sector of thought, the second displaced home of the totality became literary criticism.'[5]

Nairn took up and elaborated Anderson's thesis in a later article on the literary intelligentsia: '. . . there is', he wrote 'an intelligentsia in England, more embedded in and dispersed throughout the social body than usual; its job is the creation of a myth-world that bolsters the ailing body . . . . Literature is a main instrument in this great task; and it is doubtful if any intellectual class anywhere has ever had more natural authority and easy power.'[6]

Nairn goes on to describe what he terms a 'patrician culture', whose producers '. . . toiled willingly and responsibly to provide that societal cement without which a break in the fabric of England would have been inevitable'.[7] He presents a thumbnail sketch of this tradition, answering his own question as to why English literature was so central to it. Its most salient features were: the concept of 'the organic community', located in the countryside and in the indeterminate past, '. . . a stable society, hierarchical, yet human, nourishing to the higher sentiments . . .';[8] in the cult of individual human nature: 'Culture is the restoration of an originally better state of affairs' with respect to both the individual and society; an ideology which is anti-capitalist in tendency: 'Anti-machine, anti-money and anti-city

4

— but not anti-bourgeois. . . . English industrialization had to co-exist with the Village Green and be ruled by Gentlemen.'[9] It cultivated eccentricity, and was deeply anti-intellectual, anti-theoretical, and anti-rational. The centrality of literature Nairn explained by the nature of its self-imposed task: 'What literature does, and what abstract theorising never could do, is to evoke the organic continuities of English life by imaginative suggestion.'[10] – ie only an illusion

In the course of the analysis there was a shift. Where Anderson had denigrated the failure of the English bourgeoisie to produce a totalizing theoretical ideology, Nairn is more inclined to recognize the strengths it gained from its very prag-matism and lack of system. But whatever strengths this cultural complex may have had in the past Nairn, in *The Break-Up of Britain*, saw these as well and truly spent in mid-twentieth cen-tury Britain.

One feature of the great tradition of literary criticism, and the English intelligentsia, which was perhaps too obvious to be noticed by Anderson and Nairn in the pre-feminist sixties is its near complete domination by men. The political elite is exclu-sively male, and the affinal literary elite contains only a sprink-ling of women. The very listing of members by their second names is telling — only women require the identifying prefix or forename. No doubt the women who made possible the passing on of these illustrious second names from father to son, them-selves drew on the same small pool of names as daughters and sisters. The links between the names become visible only when the exchange of women is documented, along with the change of names that this entails. There is, as Anderson implies, a strong link through marriage which strengthens class and cultural identification through the web of kinship. The female line there-fore is essential to the process but always hidden. One of the things which I wish to do in this work is to question whether the role of women in relation to this culture was restricted to their roles as wives and mothers. Later contributors to the literary cultural historiography inaugurated by Anderson and Nairn have thrown little light upon this question. The place of women within this cultural formation remains neglected.

Feminist literary theory in Britain today has been occupied by similar concerns and interests to those of the two major schools of feminist literary theory, the French and the American, which together constitute a substantial and important body of writing. But while the same texts and the same periods of English literary history have been subject to feminist and New Left scrutiny, there has been very little interchange between them. The stories that they tell lie side by side, with little cross reference or common ground. The story told in left literary historiography is *ideol* principally the story of the production and reproduction of bourgeois ideology in literary form. Its subplot tells of subversion within the text; of literary insurgency, revolution even, at the level of form. The story told by literary feminism brings this subplot to the foreground, but the covert and overt subversion it seeks to uncover relates not to the goals of socialism but to feminism.[11] It is not this latter story which primarily concerns me here, although I will be touching upon it from time to time. Rather the focus is on the place of women and of a highly differentiated gender order, in the production, reproduction and transmission of a class culture. For if class relations are, as Dorothy Smith says, 'gender-saturated', so, too, is the creation and transmission of class culture.[12] Men and women have different relationships to the major institutions of literary and ideological production. Therefore the history of women reading and women writing must be set in the context of class as well as gender. In turn, the analysis of the processes of class and culture must register the differential place within these processes of men and women. Class is too often, still, treated as though it were a relationship between men, and culture as something produced by men and transmitted to men across generations. Like the biblical account of father begetting sons, which omits the mediating body of the mother, so this cultural begetting omits her mind.

This work, then, is as much concerned with the relationship of the English novel to capitalism and class as it is with the relationship of women to the novel. It covers a broad span of the novel's history, from the last quarter of the eighteenth century, through the nineteenth, and just into the twentieth. But it does not attempt to structure that history into a continuous narrative. Rather it takes a number of key moments when the conditions of literary production were undergoing change, and explores questions of class, gender and literature in relation to these changes.

The Rise of the Novel

The next chapter might appear to stretch an already over-extended time-span by returning to an earlier period, that usually identified as the moment of birth of the English novel in the eighteenth century. However its purpose is to interrogate Ian Watt's seminal formulation of the thesis that the novel per se is essentially realist and bourgeois, and through this interrogation, to demarcate the themes and problems addressed in my book as a whole.[13] It is Watt's thesis which is under scrutiny in this chapter and not the history of the early novel. For while he develops it through an analysis of the novels of Defoe, Fielding and Richardson in the context of the transformation of the conditions of literary production and consumption by capitalism and the market, yet he explicitly claims for it a more general validity. He identifies the novel form per se with the conventions of formal realism, and these in turn with bourgeois sensibility. He speaks of '. . . the very considerable extent to which the novel in general, as much in Joyce as in Zola, employs the literary means here called formal realism'.[14] While the frame within which Watt develops his theory is more Weberian than Marxist, nevertheless the same close identification of the conventions of realism with the production and reproduction of bourgeois ideological effects may be found in more recent Marxist formulations of the thesis.[15] For one such writer for instance, 'the classic realist text' includes *The Grapes of Wrath, The Sound of Music, L'Assommoir* and *Toad of Toad Hall*.[16] They are realist by virtue of their conventions, and bourgeois ideological by virtue of the (reality) effect which it is claimed they produce. While the questions I raise in the second chapter specifically relate to Watt's thesis they are of more general relevance. I have chosen to begin with Watt, because his was the first major development of the idea; because it is accessible and widely known; and because it remains a most valuable and enjoyable essay in literary and historical analysis.

In this chapter, I identify four problem areas in Watt's thesis and argue that they are not peculiar to this particular formulation, nor to the early novels on which his analysis is based. Rather they are problems which any historical sociology of the novel must confront; firstly, the problematic status of the novelist as artist/intellectual under capitalism; secondly, the question of determining the class-position of the novelist;

thirdly, and cross-cutting the first two, the way that sex and gender are implicated in cultural constructions of class; and finally we come to the question of form. Watt identified the bourgeois novel with the conventions of formal realism. But while it is true that realist conventions as they were developed in the early novel cannot be understood outside of the structures of thought and feeling characteristic of the rising bourgeoisie, yet those structures were complex and deeply contradictory, and more diverse in their effects on literature than Watt would have us believe.

The 'founding fathers' whose fiction Watt analysed, and pace Dale Spender,[17] the 'mothers' whose fiction he ignored, founded the novel as literature, but also, necessarily, as entertainment. As Watt rightly argues, the novel is one of the earliest cultural commodities. He links its emergence in the early- to mid-eighteenth century with the shift from a system of patronage to production for an anonymous market. Its commodity status and the attendant need for popular appeal was used against the novel by its detractors, who held that there was an inherent contradiction between literature and commerce, and between literary value and popular appeal.

In so far as novelists wished to acquire the mantle of 'literature' they were constrained to work within the conventions of realism, since literary value became early identified in fiction with realism — an identification that was not effectively challenged until the advent of modernism at the end of the nineteenth century. The desire for literary respectability may therefore have been a powerful determinant of the emergence of conventions of realism in the early novel. Bourgeois sensibility alone cannot account for it. For the bourgeois readership showed itself equally ready and willing to consume vast quantities of fantasy fiction when it was made available later in the eighteenth century. If literary pretension pushed the writer towards realist forms, then the more immediately pressing need to reach a willing readership may also have exerted pressure in a different direction. The novel quickly became a form of popular secular entertainment for the bourgeoisie, moving as it did so in the direction of fantasy and escapism rather than that of literary realism.

Both realist and non-realist fiction tell stories, but realist story-telling is governed by what currently passes for probable and plausible cause and effect in the social world. Non-realist story-telling recognizes different constraints. And if the goal of realism is 'to show things as they really are',[18] or, if you will, to produce the illusion of reality, then other criteria besides narrative plausibility are likely to be in play. Watt discusses some of them. Authenticity is, for him, the keynote of the realist novel. But authenticity requires a careful contextualization of the narrative in space and time. It commits the novelist to description as well as narration, and lengthy description has the effect of holding back the narrative. In fantasy and escapist fiction the narrative is under no such constraint. In gothic fiction, one narrative tumbles into another in riotous excess. The popularity of the novel must surely be linked to the development of compelling narratives which carry the reader through to the end and back to the circulating library for more? The pleasure of even realist fiction is surely not only the pleasure of recognition, but also that of following a story to find out what happens next?

Entertaining Fiction, Popular Form, and 'the Ladies': 1770-1820

The first period singled out in this book, discussed in chapter 3, lasted roughly from 1770-1820. It was one which saw the early rapid expansion of novel production and consumption. The fortunes of the novel then and subsequently were closely bound to those of the commercial circulating library which began to play a prominent role in its dissemination at this point in time.

It was a period during which the literary credentials of the novel were at their lowest point. It was denounced not only for its lack of literary merit, but also for its alleged effects on morals. The moral panic it occasioned in the last quarter of the eighteenth century was merely the first of a series which occurred whenever a new cultural commodity made its debut. It was repeated in very similar terms in the twentieth century over cinema and then television, both of which were attacked as culturally debased and as tending to corrupt.

The novel was attacked in literary journals, and in a wide range of writings of all kinds. 'Expressions of opinion about the dangers of novel reading pervade the ephemeral literature of the day — the little-known periodicals, books of conduct designed for young men and women, treatises on education, and even the forgotten novels themselves — as well as the letters and diaries.'[19] The fears invoked in the twentieth century over film and television focused on their effects on children and young people. In the case of the novel, it was specifically young women who were held to be most at risk. The literary, as well as the moral, critique of the novel highlighted the role of women in the production and consumption of fiction. *The Monthly* wrote in 1773, 'This branch of the literary *trade* appears now, to be almost entirely engrossed by the Ladies.'[20] The double slur against the novel is neatly combined here. The label 'trade' undermines the qualifying adjective, while its supposed engrossment by 'the Ladies' confirms its literary worthlessness. The charge behind the assertion that women were swamping the market with third rate fiction, was not so much that there were more women writers of novels than men, but that there were too many. A far far smaller number would have been quite sufficient to cause dismay, and a sense of invasion.

The proportion of readers who were women may also have been exaggerated, yet there can be no doubt that women as readers created a level of demand which acted as a major stimulant to the fiction industry from the first. Those who attacked the novel as poor literature, as well as those who drew attention to its moral dangers, were alike influenced by the belief that the novel was in some sense a feminine form, one particularly adapted to women's interests both as writers and as readers. The general grounds of attack from a literary point of view, were that the novel lacked any established tradition as a literary genre. As a result it was a form at which anyone could have a try. The novel was popularly regarded as something that could be dashed off as a pastime, or to divert attention from toothache. '... as writers of fiction, women encountered even more opposition than they had suffered as readers, and one of the major objections raised against the novel was that as a form easy to write and possessed of no traditional technique, it could be dashed off by any lady ...'.[21] At best she was patronized: 'A female author is generally, at least, a wit; and sure to produce lively and sprightly, if not very solid things.'[22] The fact that it was light and inconsequential made it 'well adapted to female ingenuity',[23] and the fact that women succeeded in this form merely confirmed its intrinsic lack of literary seriousness.

The moral attack on the novel focused on women as readers.

The easy, seductive pleasures of novel-reading would, it was feared, drive out good literature which required greater efforts on the part of the reader. The moral danger attached to novel reading, seen as an addiction, was linked to the amount of time 'wasted' in reading them: 'Asserting that the injunction regarding the proper use of time is "of a commanding nature" and "ought to have almost, if not altogether, an equal influence on our mind with 'Thou shalt do no murder,'" a Methodist observer ... (estimated) ... If two hours are spent daily with these books ... the sum is equal to "a loss of *two months* in each year; and this, in fifty years, makes an awful total of *eight years and four months* of precious time!"'[24] Even more serious was the misdirection of young women's ideas and hopes given by the novel's depiction of romantic love and courtship. It was feared that novel-reading would bring about 'a ruinous discontent on the part of the young women' ... 'a dissatisfaction on the part of the "reading Miss" with the life about her'.[25] Novel-reading, along with a superficial education in polite accomplishments, would unfit young women for their domestic lives as wives, mothers and servants.

The first period of the novel's expansion also saw a shift away from realism and the emergence of non-realist forms. In particular it witnessed the rise of gothic fiction, the dominant form of the novel from about 1790-1810. Gothic has been relatively neglected within literary critical history, which has tended to focus on the realist 'great tradition', and even at times to define the novel in terms of realism, as we have seen in the case of Watt. However as David Punter rightly claims, gothic fiction must be understood as a bourgeois form, like the realist novel analysed by Watt.[26] He brings out the paradox of a class embracing a form of fiction which in so many ways went against the grain of, even at times fundamentally violating, its own most cherished values. An attempt has been made here to explain this paradox by relating it to a contradiction central to cultural commodity production rooted in the nature of capitalism itself. Capitalist commodity consumption requires the controlled release of pleasures that may be channelled through the purchase of commodities. This is especially true of those commodities which, as Marx put it, cater to the fancy rather than the stomach.[27] While we are speaking of a time long in advance of modern consumer capitalism, nevertheless the novel may be viewed as a type of commodity which embodied a contradiction which only became apparent in the age of mass consumption.[28] Because it caters to 'the fancy', the pleasures it draws upon and releases, or promises to supply, are far removed from the classic bourgeois virtues inscribed in the idealized figure of the capitalist producer. The 'protestant ethic' which Watt finds inscribed in the early novel, is an ethic of denial, restraint, deferred gratification. It is these virtues which Punter sees as violated in the gothic fiction which the bourgeois readership nevertheless found to be so pleasurable.

The Novel, Literature, and Middle-Class Respectability: 1840-94

The second period, which forms the subject matter of chapter 4, lasted from about 1840-94. It was the period during which the novel's respectability regarding both its literary status and bourgeois values was established. It was marked by the development of a stable system of production and distribution, dominated still by the commercial circulating library, but a library grown respectable like its staple stock in trade. The key institution in this system was Mudie's Select Library, and the buying-power it commanded gave its proprietor, Charles Mudie, almost dictatorial powers over the literary fiction industry. It was a period which saw the emergence for the first time of a substantial working-class readership, but this clientele was served in the main outside the system within which the middle-class novel was produced and distributed.[29] Fiction was differentiated along class lines, with 'literary' fiction being associated with bourgeois respectability, and also with realism.

To gain recognition as 'literature' a novel had to make its first appearance in the three-decker library edition. The novelist who commanded a wider readership might appear initially in part publication or in serial form in one of the many literary magazines, particularly those run by the major publishing houses. The novel which did not appear in three-decker format, or which Mudie declined to purchase, had little chance of success. The publication of 'literary' novels was monopolized by a small number of quality publishers, and the sale at a high price to the library permitted a modestly profitable venture on the part of the publisher, on small print runs.[30]

This period also saw the return to dominance with the literary novel of realism. It was this period which produced almost all of the reconstructed 'great tradition' which became the object of English studies in the twentieth century.[31] The romantic movement in art and literature had generated in continental Europe a current whose chief object was to shock the bourgeoisie.[32] But the conditions under which the literary novel was produced and distributed in Britain in the nineteenth century ensured that it was distinctly unshocking. In fact a shortlist of those English novels which did provoke scandal would provide a measure of the extent to which the English novel allowed no place for this particular form of the revolt of bourgeois sons. The reason may have had more to do with the conditions of literary production and distribution than with Victorian prudery.

The Growth of English Studies

The entry of English onto the curriculum, particularly in institutions of higher education, provides the frame for chapter 7. The process began in the middle of the nineteenth century, and was not completed until Oxbridge was persuaded to admit the upstart discipline in the course of the twentieth century.[33] Initially it was poetry that was studied. The novel did not gain a secure place on the curriculum until the 1930s. When it did so, the long path from commodity to literature was finally traversed. The fight to place it there was at one and the same time a process of identifying and defining 'the great tradition'.

The institutionalization of English literature within the education system helped to create an expanded and differentiated market for fiction. It would be wrong to conceptualize this in terms of commercial versus non-commercial fiction. The literary novel remained and remains a commodity. The study of literature in schools and colleges stimulated the market for literary novels, and perhaps provided readers ready to exchange the pleasures of narrative, developed at their mothers knees, for the more consciously acquired pleasures of modernist texts. For from the end of the nineteenth century or thereabouts, the reign of realism was over. Literary value was increasingly sought and found in texts which broke with the earlier conventions. Realism continued to flourish. But it was no longer able to offer itself as the necessary form of literary fiction. It continued to dominate other sections of the increasingly differentiated market, particularly that section usually referred to as a 'middlebrow'.

The entry of English onto the curriculum was coterminous with the entry of women into higher education, and English, along with modern languages, is the subject they have made their own.[34] Yet in spite of this predominance of women right up through to undergraduate level, the composition of university English departments makes it very clear that this is after all a man's subject. It is by and large the best men coming up through the education system and specializing in the study of English who are channelled up to the top of the academic hierarchy. The women are somehow channelled into the lower reaches of cultural transmission. They have been recruited in force to what Gramsci termed 'the administrative levels' of cultural production,[35] above all, as teachers of humanities in schools. Clearly there are some powerful cooling-out mechanisms in play to achieve this reversal. But the question has attracted remarkably little attention from educational theorists or from historians of English studies. In the absence of closer scrutiny, it is beyond the scope of this book to identify the exact nature of these cooling-out mechanisms. But however it is done, it seems that women play an analogous role in the transmission of what Bourdieu terms 'cultural capital'[36] to the one which they play in the transmission of the more solid material variety from father to son. They enable the passing on of what is rarely theirs in their own right. The transmission of a literary culture from generation to generation depends on women: on their wholesale induction into that culture; but under the tutelege of men who remain its custodians and primary producers, as surely as does the transmission of private property to legitimate male heirs.

Literature and Ideology

The changing conditions of literary production and consumption and their effects on the novel constitute one major theme which runs through this book. A second interwoven idea pursues the question of the novel's ideological bearings. This theme runs through the entire book, but in chapters 5 and 6 the emphasis is on a point in time at which ideological questions surfaced more explicitly than is usually the case. The nineteenth-century women's movement helped provoke, and was symptomatic of, an ideological crisis over demarcations of gender in their relationship to social class. Its effects upon literary fiction were profound. On the whole, feminist and feminist-related fiction produced no revolution of form. Rather it stimulated a late flowering of realism and naturalism. The names which are remembered are Hardy, Gissing and Meredith. The women whose novels were runaway best sellers are forgotten, or are being rediscovered in the context of a new wave of feminism. Chapters 5 and 6 attempt to uncover the socio-logic of the transformation of feminism in fiction.

But ideological questions are not limited to these two chapters. Again, Watt provided a useful point of departure, although he doesn't use the language of the theory of ideology. For Watt, the realist novels he analyzed for their 'world-view' were saturated through and through by Weber's spirit of capitalism:[37] in their themes and concerns but above all in their conventions and forms. His explanation for this was simple. They were written by and for the bourgeoisie.

There have been many subsequent variants of this thesis which owe a more direct debt to Marx, and which are considerably more sophisticated. But they share the basic assumption that if capitalism produced the novel, the first form of commodity literature, then in producing it, it served capitalism's own ideological needs. But if the novel was the product of capitalism, does it follow that it was destined to serve it by producing what capitalism needed from the point of view of ideology? The answer to this question in the history of left literary critical theory has varied. Lukacs said no, and gave the realist novel of nineteenth-century Europe up to 1848 a privileged place in the production not of ideology, but of knowledge: knowledge of the hidden underlying structures of capitalist social relations.[38] He believed this in spite of the fact that fictional narratives remained on the surface of that world, with its phenomenal forms. He located the ability of realist fiction to uncover hidden structures in its formal organization as narrative rather than in themes and descriptions. It was in its overall structure of climax and resolution rather than in surface resemblances, and through 'typicality', that the great realist novel was enabled to 'tell the truth' about capitalism. There is no extended discussion of realism within this book, for the simple reason that I have already written about it at length in *Pictures of Reality* where an account of Lukacs's theory of realism may be found.[39]

Althusser, too, in spite of his distance from Lukacs in most matters, makes a distinction between 'great art' and ideology and allows the former to transcend ideological practice, to come into a somewhat obscure relationship with 'theoretical practice' or knowledge.[40] Raymond Williams, in reconstructing 'the great tradition' from a socialist perspective, aligns himself with Lukacs's disciple, Lucien Goldmann on this matter.[41] But the consensus at the present time among Marxist literary theorists is probably more nearly represented by the iconoclasm of Terry Eagleton. In *Literary Theory*[42] he asks 'what is literature?' and relentlessly exposes the inadequacies of the answers that have been offered within various schools of literary theory. He concludes that literature does not exist outside its construction within the practice of literary criticism, a practice which he firmly identifies as ideological.

This book remains agnostic about this question. But for the record, I do not believe that the case for levelling out distinctions of literary value has been proved. The question is rightly being placed once more on the agenda by writers such as Janet Wolff.[43] It is possible to identify the ideological bearings of literature without removing all of its literary claims. I have argued that the novel as a literary commodity indeed has its roots in the transformation of art and literature effected by the advent of capitalism, but that its relationship to capitalism and to the ideologies of capitalism is complex. Capitalism's ideologies are plural and discordant.

The Two Faces of Capitalist Ideology

Ian Watt foregrounded capitalism's own preferred self-image in drawing for his analysis of the realist novel on Max Weber's portrait of the Protestant businessman, and it is true that it is this most moral face which is so often visible in realist fiction. It is also the face which has been most often studied by left theorists of bourgeois ideology. Capitalism requires at one and the same time a unified subject who inhabits a sober, predictable world, and has a stable self-identity; who clocks on and off with a certain degree of predictable regularity; who likes to call a spade a spade and who believes that the term has an unproblematic and transparent relationship to the object with which the garden is dug. Much recent Marxist analysis of literary realism has concerned itself with the way in which this type of subject is 'interpellated' in this literature, in accordance with capitalism's needs.[44]

But capitalism equally needs a different kind of subject in those moments of leisure/pleasure which punctuate the working life. The self most open to infatuation with the wares of the capitalist market place is not the unified self modelled on the protestant ethic which bourgeois ideology has been said to foster and produce. It is a self which feels at home and comfortable in a world in which 'all that is solid melts into air'.[45] The novel is deeply implicated in this fracture within capitalism's imaginary selves. The nineteenth-century realist novel had its face turned towards both poles. It produced, as it had to under conditions of commodity capitalism, narratives which entertained, and which in entertaining, opened up attractive and even frightening prospects outside of the ordered regularity of a mundane bourgeois world. But it framed these narratives within a plot and an authorial voice which reaffirmed the moral values of that world. The fantasy fiction discussed in chapter 3 was even more vertiginous, but negotiated its relationship to ideology rather differently.

Just as women stand in a sex-specific relationship to literary production and consumption, so do they when viewed in relationship to capitalism's ideological needs. On the one hand it was bourgeois woman in the nineteenth century who was expected to be the public emblem of bourgeois virtue. From her allotted pedestal she was made to bear the full weight of Victorian puritanism and righteousness. On the other hand, excused from an active role in capitalist production with her exclusion from a working role in the family business, she retreated with her children to the suburbs as the family fortunes prospered. There she was placed in charge of the organization of consumption for the entire family. The bourgeoisie was the first capitalist class to have access to the means of surplus consumption, and it is in surplus rather than necessary consumption that 'all that is solid melts into air'. Rosalind Williams describes the fantasia of the Parisian department store in the second half of the nineteenth century.[46] Those most fully able to enter its fantasy world must have been bourgeois women who could not only look in numbed fascination but who could actually purchase, though not necessarily on their own behalf.

In sum, this book is trying to do two things. It attempts to shift the focus of discussion of the ideological bearings of the English novel from the context of capitalist production to that of capitalist consumption. And it has paid as much attention to the conditions of literary production and consumption as it has to the text itself. But whether the focus is that of the literary system of production, or capitalist consumption, it has insisted that the question of sex and gender must be placed at the centre of analysis alongside that of class.

2.
Capitalism and the Novel

There is a near universal consensus among Marxist and non-Marxist theorists of literature that the novel is a bourgeois form, closely linked in its rise with the development of capitalism. There is widespread agreement, too, that realism is its most characteristic type. A number of propositions are often found together or separately in respect of this thesis. Firstly, that the novel was a literary form developed by bourgeois writers and addressed to members of their own social class. It emerged from and was deeply informed by a bourgeois view of the world. Secondly, the emergence of the novel occurred on the decline of patronage and the development of an anonymous market for literature and art. Thirdly, it implies that the novel served the ideological interests and needs of capitalism and of the dominant class of capitalism, the bourgeoisie. And fourthly, we find the view expressed that realism, in its form, its content, or both, has some kind of affinity with the sense of self and the social outlook of this newly dominant class.

The Rise of the Novel

The *locus classicus* of this thesis is Ian Watt's book of this title. Although it was written as long ago as 1957, it remains the starting point for any discussion of this question. We now have a more extended body of work which explores the relationship between literature and capitalism from a Marxist perspective, notably the work of Terry Eagleton,[1] but there is no single text which does the job performed by Watt. Precisely because his thesis is a simple one clearly stated, issues which become obscured in more sophisticated discussions stand out in relief in Watt's book.

Watt identified a number of determinants in eighteenth-century Britain which, he argued, led to or facilitated the emergence and rapid growth of the novel at this time. He echoed conventional wisdom in identifying the innovators as Defoe, Fielding and Richardson, and for this he has been roundly criticized by Dale Spender.[2] The point to notice is that his criteria were literary rather than sociological. He simply took as given established literary judgements. He asked what was novel about the novel, and answered his own question through an analysis of the conventions which he identified in the novels of these men and which he termed conventions of 'formal realism'.

Formal Realism

Watt related the conventions of formal realism to the principles of philosophical realism as these had been developed by Locke and Descartes in the seventeenth century. Belief in a reality which consisted only in individual particulars, and knowable through '... the study of the particulars of experience by the individual investigator, who, ideally at least, is free from the body of past assumptions and traditional beliefs'[3] left its mark upon the novel. Watt identified the characteristics of formal realism as follows:

i. Traditional plots were rejected in favour of plots constructed on the criterion of truth to individual experience. They were drawn from life rather than from literary precedent.

ii. Plots were acted by 'particular people in particular circumstances'.[4] These people were given proper names rather than type-names like 'Mr Badman', or names which indicate situation, like 'Perdita'. Like real people in the real social world, they were in possession of consciousness and memory.

iii. The past experiences of characters in the novel were the cause of present actions. Narrative cause and effect was traced through the actions, interactions, experience and consciousness of characters.

iv. The action of the plot was located in identifiable time and space. The early novelists often used almanacs, coach timetables, histories and chronicles, to ensure the spatial and temporal authenticity of their stories. Space, the correlate of time in the identification of unique particulars according to philosophical realism, translated in the novel of formal realism into a '. . . characteristic solidity of setting'.[5]

v. Watt finds in the early novel a referential, denotational use of language which is closer to that of commonsense speech than it is to the polysemantic language of poetry; also a certain formlessness in the novel's structure — a refusal of any style which draws attention to itself, because stylishness detracts from authenticity, and authenticity is the very hallmark of formal realism. Indeed this whole array of conventions is aimed at producing the impression of authenticity to individual experience. The novel uses, according to Watt, similar criteria of truth to those of a court of law; the attitude invited from the reader is not unlike that of a juror towards a witness.

In linking formal realism in the novel to philosophical realism, Watt is not postulating any direct connection between them, but rather a common cause in the changing sense of self and of the world which was emerging at that time in the experience and outlook of the bourgeoisie. The individualism which both embody is the atomistic individualism of classical political economy, and all three are intellectual products of market capitalism. Watt drew on the work of Max Weber for his account of the psychic and cultural transformation attendant upon capitalism, of which the class of capitalist entrepreneurs was the bearer. Weber located the source of 'the spirit of capitalism' in the ethical imperatives of certain protestant sects rather than in the quotidien routines of capitalism itself.[6] Watt argues that this 'spirit of capitalism' and the development of formal realism in the novel, were mediated by the transformation of the conditions of literary production and consumption which took place in the eighteenth century as literature itself came into the orbit of capitalist production.

Conditions of Literary Production

The reading public did not extend beyond the middle class, because only at this level or above were to be found the necessary prerequisites for extensive reading; sufficient leisure, surplus income over and above that required for the purchase of bare necessities, and an adequate level of literacy. Watt recognized that access to the novel was extended through circulating libraries and the practice of communal reading, and that some sectors of the working class may have been novel-readers — he mentioned in particular female servants. But the class which provided the bulk of the novel's readership and which sustained the market for novels was the expanding bourgeoisie, and within that class, women as they withdrew from involvement in the day to day running of the business enterprise to become 'ladies' of (apparent) leisure.

The role of the upper-class patron of the arts was being superseded by a range of capitalist producers and intermediaries, such as printers, booksellers, critics and reviewers, as literature came under the sway of market forces. As part of the bourgeoisie to whose taste the new form catered, booksellers and printers were well-placed, argued Watt, to assess novels for their market appeal. 'By virtue of their multifarious contacts with printing, bookselling, and journalism, Defoe and Richardson were in very direct contact with the new interests and capacities of the reading public; but it is even more important that they themselves were wholly representative of the new centre of gravity of that public. As middle-class London tradesmen they had only to consult their own standards of form and content to be sure that what they wrote would appeal to a large audience.'[7]

Watt's thesis, then, proposed a tight interconnection between three phenomena, all directly or indirectly themselves a function of the development of capitalism: the conventions of formal realism which he found to be characteristic of the early novel; the values and mental attitudes of the rising bourgeoisie which he characterized in terms of Max Weber's account of the spirit of capitalism; and the shift in literary production to the commodity form, produced for an anonymous middle-class readership.

I shall argue that his characterization of all three must be questioned. The interconnection he made holds good only so long as his characterization of the things connected is accepted. While the main argument of his thesis attributing the nature and development of the novel to capitalism may be allowed to stand, the exact nature of that relationship was more complex and fractured than Watt's specification allows.

Some Problems in the Thesis

Problems of 'Formal Realism'

Watt's templet of 'formal realism' is too constrictive even for those realist novels he analyses. He has considerable difficulty with them where they manifestly do not conform to one or another of the conventions of formal realism. Fielding, for example, uses type-names, an intrusive narrative style, and much comic contrivance. Watt views these departures from formal realism with a jaundiced eye, as '... tending to compromise the narrative's general air of literal authenticity'.[8] Watt runs into a problem here which is common to many writers who wish to claim a special relationship between the novel, realism, and bourgeois ideology. Either a very broad definition of realism is used, such that the vast majority of novels may be included within its terms. This is the effect of MacCabe's definition of 'classic realism'.[9] Or a narrower and more useful definition of realism is offered which singles out a particular type of fiction, but this type is then used to define the novel per se. Any fiction which does not fit the definition is excluded as not a novel in the full sense. This second strategy is followed by Watt in his thesis. Because he is dealing with the early, formative years of the novel's history, he is able to deploy the argument that any exceptions are simply due to the as yet imperfect crystallization of the form and its conventions. Fielding's departures from formal realism are understood by Watt as mistakes which Fielding himself '... seems to have realized ... by the time he came to write his last novel ...'[10] Had Fielding written further novels we must suppose, if we follow Watt, that his fiction would have increasingly converged with that of Defoe and Richardson in recognizing and respecting the rules of formal realism.

Sterne is accounted for in different terms. *Tristram Shandy* is characterized as a parody of the novel, which, in its reduction to absurdity of the conventions of formal realism, backhandedly confirms that these conventions indeed define the novel. This special pleading by Watt has a certain plausibility with respect to the early novel. But it has none when it comes to later fiction which also departs from the conventions identified by Watt: Dickens, with his use of type-names and comic implausiblity in the manner of Fielding; or Trollope, Thackeray or Meredith, with their prominent authorial intrusion. Watt falls back on appeals to authority: '... Henry James was shocked by the way Trollope, and other "accomplished novelists", concede "in a digression, a parenthesis or an aside" that their fiction is "only make-believe"'.[11] It is clear that what began as a descriptive category used to characterize the conventions which were, as a matter of fact, followed by the early novelists, has become a prescription. A 'proper' novel obeys the rules delineated by Watt under the head of formal realism, and the early novelists may be seen struggling to establish these rules. But once established, then any refusal to conform is roundly condemned by Watt as bad literary practice. What began as a neutral description of conventions actually followed in the main, has become a literary obligation which the novelist refuses on peril of producing work which is seriously flawed as a result. This is an instance of Watt's tendency to conflate sociological and literary criteria. As a literary critic he is perfectly entitled to make such judgements. But in offering a sociological explanation for the rise of the novel, he must explain the novel as it was and not as he might have liked it to be.

In addition to forcing Watt to use literary criteria to exclude practices which do not fit his sociological explanation, while dealing with novelists who fall within the broad tradition of realism, his templet also leads him to ignore all other traditions within the novel. He simply does not discuss gothic fiction, yet gothic followed very closely upon the heels of the early novel. The exact location of Udolpho in space and time is not determinable not because Ann Radcliffe had not fully learnt the rules governing the novel, but because it is irrelevant. Neither can gothic be excluded on the grounds that it was not a bourgeois form. It was immensely popular among precisely the bourgeois reading public identified by Watt with the fiction of realism.

If we want to uncover the history of the novel in its social context, we must consider a whole range of types, not all of which are governed by the conventions of formal realism. And if the rising bourgeoisie had an elective affinity of some kind with the realist novel, then its taste extended to other, radically different types of novel.

The Novel, the Bourgeoisie and the Spirit of Capitalism

a) Social Class and Authorship. Knowledge of the class origins of the novelist does not in and of itself explain the form and content of the novel. The bourgeoisie is and was a heterogeneous class in terms of income, style of life, and cultural pretensions. Moreover novel-writing alone does not determine class position. Or rather, as Eagleton puts it, '. . . the individual class-position of a literary producer . . . may be in contradiction with his mode of insertion into the class-structure *as an author'*.[12] Structurally, the author is a petty-bourgeois producer. Yet novel-writing may be combined with a number of other occupations which are indicative of class position. Richardson and Defoe, master-printer and journalist/jack-of-all-trades respectively, present one set of conceptual problems. Here at least there is a relative homogeneity of class position and authorship. Fielding, lawyer and traditional intellectual, is another matter, while Austen, clergyman's daughter with connections with the lesser gentry, is another again. However the question which Eagleton forces and which Watt evades, is whether and to what extent the structural position of the author as petty-producer of literary manuscripts binds her/him into a specific relationship with capitalist society irrespective of any other determinants of class membership which the author may possess.

My initial point of departure in considering this question, was, like that of Anderson and, following his lead, Eagleton, Gramsci's theory of intellectuals. Throughout the successive redraftings of this work I have moved further and further away from this point of departure. But Gramsci has been so very influential for the architects of new left literary theory in this country that a brief consideration of his theory is necessary. The concepts which are most relevant here are those of 'traditional' and 'organic' intellectuals, and it is worth quoting in full the passage where he defines these two types, in the context of a tantalizingly brief passage on 'the peculiarities of the English': 'In England the development is very different from France. The new social grouping that grew up on the basis of modern industrialism shows a remarkable economic-corporate development but advances only gropingly in the intellectual-political field. There is a very extensive category of organic intellectuals — those, that is, who come into existence on the same industrial terrain as the economic group — but in the higher sphere we find that the old land-owning class preserves its position of virtual monopoly. It loses its economic supremacy but maintains for a long time a politico-intellectual supremacy and is assimilated as "traditional intellectuals" and as directive [dirigente] group by the new group in power. The old landowning aristocracy is joined to the industrialists by a kind of suture which is precisely that which in other countries unites the traditional intellectuals with the new dominant classes.'[13]

The categories of traditional and organic intellectuals are themselves relatively clear, at least in the abstract. Organic intellectuals who '. . . come into existence on the same industrial terrain' as the new class, have a relationship to that class which is fairly transparent. Examples might be trades union leaders in relationship to the working class, or managerial elites and the bourgeoisie. For traditional intellectuals, the relationship is less transparent, because such strata were already in existence prior to the emergence of the new mode of production. They had access to and control over institutions such as the church, university and legal system, which gave them some measure of independence and they are characterized by Gramsci in terms of a strong corporate identity and *esprit de corps* which that independence sanctioned. Their relationship to the social order and its ruling class therefore has the appearance of being open to negotiation. Gramsci argues that the traditional intellectuals are in reality no more than the organic intellectuals of an earlier epoch, and that they, too, are intellectuals of capitalism, but their relationship to capitalism is more mediated and obscured than that of the organic intellectuals. The most typical traditional intellectuals would be the ecclesiastic, the lawyer and the scholar/teacher: all those in fact who usually fall under commonsense definitions of that term. These traditional intellectuals present and experience themselves as detached and relatively autonomous, with no necessary allegiance to the dominant class or the new order. While Gramsci goes on to demystify this appearance, he backhandedly confirms it at the same time in his contention that the traditional intellectuals must be 'won over' to the new regime, and that this is the principal task facing its organic intellectuals. Traditional intellectuals see themselves as the natural custodians of cultural values and standards, to whose judgements on such matters the holders of mere economic power should defer.

In the brief passage quoted above, Gramsci suggested that British capitalism experienced some considerable difficulty in generating organic intellectuals of sufficient stature to succeed in this task of winning over traditional intellectuals to capitalism, and this was the theme that Anderson developed and expanded in his work on English class culture. Gramsci's is a functionalist argument, and it assumes that a unified, homogeneous culture is what capitalism best needs. In the debate which Anderson initiated, another possibility emerged. Summarizing the debate, Richard Johnson cast the very lack of homogeneity of that culture as a strength rather than a weakness: 'So it came about that the first working class whose theories, forms of organization and strategies had, in any case, to be improvised from the start, faced always a double armoury: the economic power of manufacture *and* farmer/landlord; the ideologies of deference *and* of self-help; High Tory Anglicanism *and* militant Dissent or popular anti-Catholicism. . . .'[14] I shall come back to this question in the next section of this chapter, to argue that this heterogeneity was not just a historical accident, but that capitalism itself generates and produces a necessary heterogeneity in its culture.

Meanwhile to return to the class position of the novelist: while Gramsci's pair of concepts may be insufficient to classify all of capitalism's intellectuals, it is very useful when considering the ways in which intellectuals viewed themselves.

The system of patronage by church, state and aristocracy which preceded the period in which art and literature became commodities left the direct producer in little doubt as to her/his dependence upon the representatives of the dominant class of society. It fostered not so much the *esprit de corps* which Gramsci associated with the traditional intellectual, and a self-perception of independence and autonomy, as the image of a special kind of higher servant or skilled craftsman. Paradoxically it was only with the decline of patronage and the transformation of art and literature by commodity production that there emerged among this stratum a conception of the artist/literary producer akin to that which Gramsci attributed to the traditional intellectual. This change is especially clear in the case of the painter, and can be seen in the changing styles of self-portraiture during the course of the eighteenth century.[15] During the eighteenth century and especially in the older arts and literary forms, the identity of the cultural producer began to crystallize around a set of institutions that came to define and constitute the 'art worlds' of contemporary capitalism.[16] The artistic producer was an individual creator, a 'genius'. This individuation of the cultural producer, along with the concept of creative genius, was to provide the soil for romanticism which came increasingly to define artistic production in the era of industrial capitalism. It implied a certain distance between the producer and her/his social class, and emphatically denied any service role towards the capitalist state and its ruling class. Increasingly, and under the impact of romantic thought, high culture producers came to see themselves as belonging to a natural elite or aristocracy of creative genius who might in principle be recruited from any social class but who as a matter of fact, ironically, were very often bourgeois sons.[17] They saw themselves as custodians of aesthetic and intellectual values far removed from the cash nexus of a bourgeois-capitalist world in which they were systematically devalued. The true creative artist was necessarily alienated, an outsider, a species of disaffected traditional intellectual.

The situation of the novelist however was rather different to that of the older creative artist. The novel came into existence as a commodity. Commodity production was not, as it was for older forms already in existence prior to this development, something alien to which it had with difficulty to adapt, but a condition of its very existence. Its producer might therefore be expected to look with a less jaundiced eye upon capitalism and the dominant class of capitalism, the bourgeoisie, which provided its readership. If Watt is correct, then this was indeed the case. But by the same token, and precisely to the extent that the novel defined itself as a commodity, the newly emerging 'traditional art worlds' refused to recognize its claims as literature. The new child of capitalist literary production was greeted by the world of letters with scandalized opprobrium. So universally were the novel and novel-reading condemned that novelists themselves joined in the chorus. Jane Austen, writing at a time when the literary fortunes of the novel were beginning to turn, could caricature the earlier self-denigration of the novel in fiction: 'I will not adopt that ungenerous and impolitic custom so common with novel writers, of degrading by their contemptuous censure the very performances, to the number of which they are themselves adding . . .. Alas! If the heroine of one novel be not patronized by the heroine of another, from whom can she expect protection and regard? ... Let us not desert one another; we are an injured body.'[18]

The novelist, then, might appear to be a promising candidate for the role of organic intellectual of capitalism. If Defoe and Richardson, the two authors above all on whom Watt rests his case, were typical, coming as they did from the trading and commercial strata, then the case for so regarding them is additionally strengthened. But there is at least one small difficulty. The space into which the novel was born, newly created it is true, was nevertheless 'always already occupied' as the saying goes, by literature. But the arbiters of literary value judged the eighteenth-century novel and on the whole found it wanting. The new child was declared illegitimate. As the introduction shows, traditional intellectuals as well as critics and reviewers attacked the novel as morally pernicious and aesthetically worthless. This placed the novelist in a weak position so far as concerned the heroic task assigned by Gramsci to the organic intellectual, that of winning over the traditional intellectuals to the cause of capitalism. On the contrary, the novel could play no major ideological role until it had proved its literary credentials in terms of criteria determined by a literary critical elite which placed itself outside, and at a critical distance from, the new regime. The novel had to win a place on terrain marked out for literature, and it did not succeed in doing so with any degree of security until the early decades of the nineteenth century. Kathleen Tillotson identifies the eighteen forties as the period in which the novel became the dominant literary form in Britain.[19] To become so it had to show that it could rise above its dubious origins in the literary market-place, above its function as 'mere entertainment' to claim a legitimate place as literature. To the extent that the novel succeeded in overcoming the early disapprobation it provoked, and was established as literature, so the novelist moved closer to the stance of the traditional intellectual, a stance distanced from capitalism and commerce, and claiming the right to be critical. Hence the often noted tendency in the English novel towards anti-capitalism.[20] As the novel became more integrated into the literary art world, so its attitude toward capitalism became more measured. Because of his focus on the early novel, Watt overemphasized the extent to which the novel unproblematically reproduced the values of market capitalism.

b) The Spirit of Capitalism. If we look at the response in France to the commoditization of literature, we find a more thoroughgoing hostility to capitalism and even to the bourgeoisie itself. For the French romantics, the function of art and literature could not be further removed from those which Gramsci ascribed to organic intellectuals. They were inclined to see the task not as the mobilization of consent for the new order, but on the contrary, *pour epater le bourgeois.*[21] In the early nineteenth century Alfred de Musset wrote 'Damned Be the Family, and Society. Cursed be the Home and Cursed Be the City. Damnation upon the Motherland.'[22] Mario Praz speaks of the romantics '... conscious and pleasurable violation of the normal'.[23] The normal which they violated was bourgeois normality, bourgeois values. Graña explains this revolt of bourgeois sons in the same terms in which Watt explains the bourgeois realism of the early English novel. The root cause, identified by both for their chosen explanations, was the dislocation of traditional forms of sponsorship as art became a commodity, subject as such to the laws of the capitalist market place. How could two such opposed effects be produced by the same cause?

Gaunt argues that romanticism was a product of the aftermath of the French revolution and the Napoleonic wars.[24] Watt was writing of Britain three-quarters of a century or so earlier, and thanks to Anderson and Nairn, we are all now sensitive to the peculiarities of the English — the time scales are different to those of continental Europe. Nevertheless it is difficult to reconcile these two accounts of such widely differing responses to the commercialization of art and literature. In the face of this disparity, what is required is a re-thinking of received ideas about bourgeois ideology and the ideological needs and characteristics of capitalism.

The history of the bourgeoisie in nineteenth- and twentieth-century Britain and elsewhere, suggests that the bourgeois self may find the publicly sanctioned persona of the 'protestant ethic' type an increasingly uncomfortable and obsolete straitjacket in practice and under the temptations afforded by increasing affluence. And not all of the contradictory needs of capitalism are equally served by this spirit of frugality, restraint, deferred gratification, rational calculation. Bourgeois ideology has been studied until recently almost entirely from the point of view of the requirements of capitalist production and the disciplined and restrained self that participation in capitalist production generates and fosters. Max Weber's thesis, which as we have seen, heavily influenced Watt's interpretation of the early novel, constructs the 'spirit of capitalism' entirely from the point of view of the capitalist producer, constrained to plough his profits back into the enterprise. But capitalism is Janus-faced. When the capitalist producer has his eye to his own management and workforce, the qualities he likes to find and encourage are the classic bourgeois virtues — thrift, efficiency, hard work, frugality. But when he turns his attention to the purchaser of his commodities he may be happy to find a different creature, with money in wallet or purse and in a frame of mind to spend. From the point of view of consumption, repression and rational calculation are more dubious assets.

This tension between the contradictory requirements of capitalist consumption and capitalist production do not become evident until the era of consumer capitalism in the second half of the nineteenth century. But they are implicit in its logic from the start. The sale and purchase of commodities implies the controlled release of pleasures and their channelling through commodity consumption. Marx was aware of this double standard intrinsic to capitalism. '. . . each capitalist does demand that his workers should save, but only *his own* because they stand towards him as workers; but by no means the remaining *world of workers* for these stand towards him as consumers. In spite of all "pious" speeches he therefore searches for means to spur them on to consumption, to give his wares new charms, to inspire them with new needs. . . .'[25] Capitalist consumption was never integrated into Marx's general theory of capitalism. But it is evident that there is potential conflict between the imaginary selves sanctioned and fostered by church, family, school, legal system — the major ideological institutions which have commanded the attention of Marxist theories of ideology — and the imaginary selves fostered in the market-place by the proliferation of commodities. Perhaps we have taken too seriously the pious speeches emanating from these institutions? For capitalism is simultaneously transmitting another message: spend, spend, spend! This, too, is the work of ideological production, and unless both components of the national culture are laid side by side and the relationship between them brought out, we will have only a partial understanding of the nature of ideological production under capitalism.

Those ideological institutions which have provided the source of capitalism's pious speeches and which are most relevant to the ideological requirements of capitalist production, are the ones which have been staffed by traditional-style intellectuals, often non-conformist, who supplied the ranks of those vocal 'moral entrepreneurs' who attempted in the nineteenth century and since to define and regulate leisure activity in terms of rational self-improvement.[26] Their censoriousness towards the excesses of the market-place, even towards capitalism itself at times, becomes more understandable in terms of this double-face of capitalism. The 'protestant ethic' has indeed an 'elective affinity' with the spirit of capitalism, as Weber believed, but only in its more pious manifestation. The non-conformist intellectuals who came to serve the ideological interests of capitalism from within the institutional strongholds of church and school never formed a solid intellectual bloc with all of capitalism's organic intellectuals. In spite of the social and cultural differences which separated them, non-conformist intellectuals were in some respects closer in attitude to the older, traditional intellectuals associated with landed families, than they were to the 'commercial entrepreneurs' who were just as surely produced by capitalism, and whose stereotypical brashness in advertizing the charms of the capitalist's wares was a prime target of censure. The education of taste, the expansion of wants which Marx identified as essential to the development of capitalist consumption, runs counter to both traditional intellectual values, and to the values of bourgeois protestantism. Bourgeois respectability and the contingencies of capitalist production create one kind of persona, capitalist consumption another. It was the commercial entrepreneurs who proved the more adept at '... bringing leisure "needs" into line with the leisure goods that were available'.[27] Capitalism, in the long run, needed both types of entrepreneur, and a conflicting, plural ideology. The intellectual who entered the major institutions which guaranteed to intellectuals their *esprit de corps* and independence best served the interests of capitalism by maintaining the traditional intellectuals' moral distance from capitalism. The unacceptable face of capitalism could be censured by capitalism's intellectuals as though the excesses of the market had no intrinsic relationship to capitalist production and the classic bourgeois virtues it fostered and extolled. The new disciplines and activities of these moral entrepreneurs, including English studies and sociology, created the space for what might be termed 'bourgeois anti-capitalism'. Much of the history of sociological thought is coloured by precisely such an attitude.

If ideology is lived in the heart and the mind of individuals, then the question arises how this contradiction within bourgeois ideology was negotiated at the level of the individual. How are and were these contradictory selves reconciled? For the same individuals are both producers and consumers. It may be partly through the compartmentalization of work and leisure, and partly through the linking of saving with spending. Frugality becomes not so much a way of life as gratification deferred — the promise of moments of hedonism/leisure which punctuate periods of work. This simultaneous appeal to frugality and excess may be seen most graphically in contemporary advertising of banks, insurance companies and building societies who wish to attract savings. Saving is no longer offered as a virtue in itself, as it was in the irrational rationality of the Weberian model, but as a means to the end of spending. Finally the reconciliation is facilitated where there is a sharp segregation between leisure and non-leisure classes. Ideological pluralism along class lines is to a degree commensurable with the needs of capitalism. A class whose main function from the point of view of capitalism relates to consumption rather than production, does not need to be inspired by any vision of frugality and constraint. The rentier classes of eighteenth- and nineteenth-century Britain who were mainly associated with the land fall into this category, while at this same period the main function of the working class was to work, and their consumer function was limited to necessary expenditure on clothing and food which hardly required any cultivation of taste for excess. Moreover with the exception of alcohol, those forms of excess which found expression in traditional working-class leisure pursuits were not organized through the market-place, via the sale and purchase of commodities. Therefore policies aimed at regulating and eliminating bear-baiting and other such pursuits in favour of more 'rational' and self-improving activities were perfectly compatible with the consumer needs of capitalism at the time.[28] But in the long term, the workers, too, had to be wooed as consumers.

Paradoxically it was the bourgeoisie itself that experienced earliest and most acutely this contradiction between capitalist consumption and production. The pious preachings of the spirit of capitalism were primarily addressed to them — the other party to capitalist production, the worker, perhaps required no special motivation over and above the dull compulsion of necessity. But the primary bearers of the bourgeois virtues were also the first capitalist class whose income was high enough to permit surplus consumption, and who were therefore most open to the ideological effects of the capitalist market-place.

If the novel was, as Watt claims, a commodity-form of literature produced by and for the bourgeoisie, then where did it stand in relation to this double-bind of bourgeois ideology? Like the art world of French bohemian romanticism, it stood ambivalently. The romantic bohemians on the continent shared their cultural elitism and hostility to vulgar commerce with the traditional intellectuals of church and school. But their hostility was mounted not from the perspective of bourgeois respectability as it was in Britain. It was in addition anti-bourgeois, and frequently took the form, as Praz has documented, of pleasure in the violation of the normal. As such it was even more shocking to traditional intellectuals than were the antics of capitalism's commercial entrepreneurs. Praz's study traces the recurrent sado-masochistic imagery of romanticism and decadence in the nineteenth century and what better material *pour épater le bourgeois*? Another current often noted in romanticism is its exoticism. Again this can be traced back to the eighteenth century in its cultivation of the sublime in painting and literature. It carries through to the end of the nineteenth century and beyond, finding expression in Rossetti's mania for indiscriminate collecting of the *objets* which filled his house, a taste which Whistler channelled towards things oriental.[29]

The sources mined by the romantics in their search for escape from and refusal of bourgeois values paradoxically brought them back again to certain features of the capitalist market-place. Romantic exoticism was matched and outstripped by the Paris Exposition of 1900, described by a contemporary as '... a gaudy and incoherent jumble of Hindu temples, savage huts, pagodas, souks, Algerian alleys, Chinese, Japanese, Sudanese, Senegalese, Siamese, Cambodian quarters ...' and by the fantasy inscribed in the Parisian department store. The tone of the traditional intellectual may be detected in the description: '. . . a sort of "universe in a garden" of merchandise. The sheer variety, the assault of dissociated stimuli, is one cause of the numbed fascination of the customers . . . syncretism, anachronism, illogicality, flamboyance, childishness . . . an attempt to express visions of distant places in concrete terms . . . a style which may be called the chaotic exotic.'[30] The images of romanticism are repeated in the very market-place from which romanticism is an attempted escape. Similar themes and imagery recur, and pass over directly into certain fertile currents of popular culture. Horror and terror, exoticism and eroticism are staples of popular forms. Often the same sources are common to both. Baudelaire was fascinated by the tales of Edgar Alan Poe, the same tales that were to provide a goldmine for twentieth-century film scripts.

However romantic bohemianism, while it exerted a considerable fascination for cultural producers in Britain, never became institutionalized as it did in France. We do not find the same impulse to shock the bourgeois in the British national culture. But we do find an ideological dualism nevertheless. In the period from 1840-94, the period of the dominance of so-called classic realism and of the production of what was later to be canonized as the great tradition, the pole of classic bourgeois respectability and the virtues fostered in production are perhaps paramount. While in the earlier period, that of the first expansion of novel-writing and -reading from about 1770-1820, a different type of novel was dominant — one which reads today like an expurgated version of sado-masochistic pornography; the gothic novel. Bourgeois respectability on the one hand, and the exotic/erotic on the other, remain present in both types of English fiction. It would not do to make an absolutely hard and fast distinction between them. And clearly, gothic fiction was too early a development to be related directly to consumer fantasies of the kind described by Williams.[31] Rather it can be argued that the novel as commodity shared some of the characteristics of capitalist merchandise of different kinds which only became visible with the explosion of consumer capitalism at a later period in time. To repeat, capitalist consumption entails the controlled release of pleasures, and unconscious wishes must have been a potent source of pleasure appealed to both in commodity fiction and in consumer goods sold later in department stores.

Women as Intellectuals

Women as Readers

The differentiation under capitalism of two separate spheres, the public and the private, one masculine, the other feminine, was a prominent feature of the dominant symbolic order by the early nineteenth century in Britain. Feminists have rediscovered this division, and have explored the inner and outer landscapes of the private sphere, the home, within which bourgeois women were at least in theory confined. It should be emphasized that, as they emerged in the eighteenth century, both spheres were bourgeois, although defined and analysed in universal terms as if they were a function of biological sex given by nature. That these divisions were actually developed with the bourgeoisie in mind can be seen in the unselfconscious class double standard of some of this writing, where in the same passage women are ascribed quite contrary qualities when viewed as bourgeois 'ladies' and as working-class 'hands': 'The cerebral organisation of the female is far more delicate than that of a man; the continuity and severity of application needed to acquire real *mastery* in any profession, or over any science, are denied to women, and can never with impunity be attempted by them; mind and health would almost invariably break down .... It is clearly a waste of strength, a superfluous extravagance, an economic blunder, to employ a powerful and costly machine to do work which can be done as well by a feebler and a cheaper one. Women and girls are less costly operatives than men . . . .'[32]

The bourgeois public sphere emerged in Europe in the early decades of the eighteenth century, in institutions such as the coffee-house.[33] The simultaneous emergence of the bourgeois private sphere is associated with the privitization of family life — the withdrawal of the bourgeois family from public hall to (with)-drawing room, from integrated home and workplace to domestic quarters in the suburbs. This movement of separation and privatization took place at different points in time throughout the nineteenth century, as different industries, and different families within them, rose and prospered. It was neither uniform nor universal. Small family businesses which depended upon family labour continued to be important numerically and economically throughout, and this is one reason why the idea of rigidly defined and separated public and private spheres even for the bourgeoisie must be qualified.[34] In fact it is probably misleading to make an absolute separation between the two, especially where 'private' is conflated with 'personal', as in the writings of Zaretsky.[35] Interpersonal relations are ubiquitous and cannot be confined to the private sphere. They are negotiated in public as well. There are 'intermediate zones' which developed, necessarily, at the time of separation of public from private. Each sphere had its public and private faces. To use Goffman's dramaturgical metaphor,[36] there was a backstage to the public, and a frontstage to the private. Probably the most important decisions and negotiations belonging to the public sphere took place in private, while the bourgeois home itself might provide a semi-public space, open on a carefully restricted basis, to the world of politics and letters in salon culture. This semi-public sphere provided one of the few arenas in which women might gain political influence. Such a role was hazardous for those women who adopted it, and it was only open to married women.

The home, too, had its private and public fronts; backstairs, attics, cellars, as well as front-stairs, parlour, lobby.[37] The very segregation of women in the private sphere created the need, however, for another type of semi-public arena in which the transfer of daughters from one home to another could be negotiated. Jane Austen's world of assemblies, private balls, visiting and the London Season remains one of the most vivid fictional constructions of this carefully chaperoned and vetted intermediate sphere where courtship could be negotiated and within whose confines romantic love could be indulged. The institutions of courtship and the provision of space for its pursuit were a function of the shift from marriages arranged by parents in which the principal parties' had only a right of veto, to companionate marriages in which these rights were reversed, and parents held the veto.[38]

The most important condition for the development of a bourgeois private sphere was the increased profitability of the capitalist firm, beyond the point where profits allowed both for the reinvestment necessary for the firm's survival and expansion, and the release of the labour of wives and daughters. But the relationship of women to leisure time is notoriously problematic. Leisure time is defined over against work. Paradigmatically it is the time which is 'free' to be spent in activities which are unpaid, voluntary, and pleasurable. It is also the time and space of consumption rather than production.

It is obvious that consumption requires 'free time'; less obvious that it requires work which may or may not be paid, may or may not be pleasurable. Marx conceptualized the process of capitalist production in terms of his distinction between production and reproduction, the latter taking place in the home and in moments of leisure, in which the wear and tear caused by productive labour is made good, energy restored, in preparation for a further period of productive work. For Marx the value of labour-power (though not of its product) could be measured by the value of the goods and services purchased with the wage and used for purposes of reproduction. What Marx left out of account in this calculus was the labour cost of the processes of reproduction themselves; the labour involved in the acquisition and processing of subsistence commodities. It was omitted because it was so hard to see, since it was unpaid and performed by women. The problems posed for Marxism by domestic labour have been explored by Marxist feminists.[39] The debate has focused on the 'necessary labour' of reproduction: childcare, of course, cleaning, cooking, caring generally. But what might be termed 'surplus consumption' also costs labour-time to organize and facilitate. This labour, insofar as it *is* surplus labour, belongs precisely to that grey area which is almost impossible to classify as work or leisure, and in this it differs from 'housework'. Once domestic labour is identified it becomes visible as work. But the work of surplus consumption may not look like work at all. Yet the planning and production of the bourgeois home was and is inordinately time-consuming. The fact that it may give pleasure is not decisive in defining its status. The capitalist producer typically takes pride in the fact that his work is interesting and enjoyable, and that he takes it home with him at night. He would nevertheless resist the implication that it is therefore not real work. Equally its status is not determined by freedom of choice, and in any case these duties were not easily evaded in the nineteenth century among the middle classes.

The work involved in the production of middle-class gentility was visible in its results, on display in the semi-public parts of the home during the 'leisure' activities of entertaining and visiting which functioned to police these duties and enforce compliance to acceptable bourgeois standards. While the more affluent middle-class women had working-class servants to perform the more arduous physical tasks, there is some evidence that many were nevertheless kept busy to a degree and extent that puts the lie to the popular image of the idle lady of leisure.[40]

Ian Watt's assumption that bourgeois women had a near-monopoly of the increasing leisure time *of their class* in the eighteenth century, and that this is why they were such heavy novel readers is questionable even for this early period. Yet it is an assumption still made unthinkingly about women readers today. John Sutherland writes: 'In their adult book choices one suspects that the libraries keep in mind an average user who conforms to the pattern of ratepayer and voter, with a lot of leisure time: women in a word.'[41] It is doubtful whether middle-class women in the twentieth or the nineteenth century had more leisure time than middle-class men. What is true is that the ways available to them of deploying their leisure time were very much more restricted, and that the pattern of work/leisure was less differentiated for women. Women read in their leisure time because reading was cheap, and because it is a leisure activity which is most readily adapted to an undifferentiated work/leisure routine. A novel could be picked up and put down, read as and when, unlike the leisure pursuits of husbands and brothers which typically required blocks of free time which women, once married, did not usually have.

Women as Writers

A second small difficulty in supposing that the early novelists were among the organic intellectuals of capitalism is that the class background of Defoe and Richardson was simply not characteristic of the novelist in the eighteenth century. It was somewhat disingenuous of Watt to have taken these two men as almost his prototypes. Fielding and Austen, from professional backgrounds with ties to the landed gentry, were in fact more characteristic. A second respect in which Defoe and Richardson, along this time with all of the early novelists analysed by Watt, are atypical, is in their sex. Watt was aware of this. He acknowledged towards the end of his book, that 'The majority of eighteenth century novels were actually written by women. . . .'[42] This fact surely has serious implications for his thesis. For middle-class women have a different relationship than their brothers to capitalism, capitalist production, and their common social class. The available evidence suggests that women novelists in the eighteenth and nineteenth centuries were drawn from an even narrower social spectrum than were their male counterparts. It is notorious that so many of them were, like Austen and later the Brontës, clergymen's daughters. Showalter, writing of the nineteenth century, claims that 'Women novelists were overwhelmingly the daughters of the upper middle class, the aristocracy, and the professions.'[43]

The higher reaches of the legal profession as well as the established church were monopolized throughout the eighteenth century and well into the nineteenth by the younger sons of landed families: precisely that stratum identified by Gramsci as the source of British capitalism's traditional intellectuals. Latin was the language of traditional scholarship and provided, with Greek, the solid core of public school and university education which socialized traditional intellectuals of the landed classes. English was the preferred language of new non-conforming educational institutions. An education in the classics likewise divided men from women, and effectively debarred women of the gentry from participating in the functions of traditional intellectuals.

Showalter has identified, alongside educational differences, two further distinctions between male and female novelists which divided them throughout most of the nineteenth century. Women had almost no alternative means of support commensurate with their class membership; and they published their first novels and established a professional reputation at a later age. Male novelists were usually trained for some other career. This was true of course of the 'founding fathers', and Defoe began to write novels exceptionally late in life, at the age of sixty. As the novel became established, however, it became possible to support a bourgeois style of life on the basis of writing alone, and throughout the nineteenth century the average age at which those men who succeeded in making a career out of writing fiction published their first novel was twenty-five. A few writers like Trollope, combined writing with other non-literary occupations, and began their second, literary career rather later than usual. But most supplemented their income from fiction by journalism and related work. Showalter adds that university prizes additionally encouraged literary precosity in men.[44]

The pressure on men to establish some regular means of livelihood if they were not destined to inherit the land or a business enterprise would have had the effect of pressuring them to publish early. For if they failed to establish themselves in literature, then they would find themselves compelled to turn to some alternative, and, more to the point, with alternatives to turn to. 'Presumably men who could not establish themselves early as writers turned to more profitable occupations.'[45]

Women who aspired to authorship were in an altogether different situation. Their education and training, whether as daughters of the landed gentry, or of affinal groups who stocked the higher professions, or for that matter, the daughters of businessmen, was for one role only, that of wife and mother. The expectation of those women who were released from the duties of supplying family labour for small business enterprises was that they would not be responsible for supporting themselves in a profitable career, and no such careers were open to middle-class women until well into the second half of the nineteenth century. This expectation placed a substantial minority of such women in an impossible situation. If they failed or refused to marry, or if the source of male support upon which they depended dried, up, through illness, death, or financial failure, they found themselves without the means to support themselves and their dependents. Showalter suggests that many women eagerly seized the opportunity offered by financial exigency or the illness/death of breadwinners as an excuse to do what they would have liked to do in any case: '. . . the invalid mother, the bankrupt father, the tubercular husband, and the errant son are wheeled out by demure authoresses in whose downcast eye we can detect the glint of steely purpose'.[46]

But whether forced into writing by the stick of financial necessity, or lured by the carrot of literary ambition, women would typically find themselves in a position to consider a literary career at a number of stages in the life-cycle and not just in the early years, like their brothers. One category of women who were very likely to find themselves in the position where a literary career might seem both possible and desirable was the daughters of younger sons of gentry families. Younger sons typically entered the church, the law and the armed forces. Their inheritance being more modest than that of the favoured eldest, such families were very likely to find themselves unable to provide sufficiently sizeable marriage portions for their daughters, to secure marriages commensurate with their status. It is no accident that so many women novelists in the nineteenth century and earlier were the daughters of clergymen. In other words, women writers were drawn to an even greater extent than their male counterparts from the class that supplied Gramsci's traditional intellectuals. The sons of a Church of England clergyman were likely to follow the career patterns of Jane Austen's brothers, who entered the church themselves, or gained commissions in the army and navy through the exercise of patronage on their behalf by wealthier landed kin. The daughters, insofar as they had any occupation outside of marriage, could only become governesses or writers. Patronage could not be exercised so effectively to secure wealthy husbands of their class, as it could be for their brothers to secure a church living or a commission in the navy. For where marriage was concerned, a good portion weighed more than good connections. These women were competing on a marriage market which was still, as Moll Flanders had complained, 'overstocked'. They competed at a disadvantage not only with better portioned women of their own class, but also with wealthy city heiresses of less 'good birth'.

While their lack of cash and marriagability may have made a career desirable, their class background made it likely that they might succeed in writing. For while women were relatively disadvantaged compared to their brothers in the matter of education, the daughters of traditional intellectuals might find themselves better educated, and better supplied with 'cultural capital' than other women. Nevertheless the daughters of tradesmen and businessmen who failed or refused to marry, or found themselves for whatever reasons without means of support, faced the same restricted set of choices. They could become governesses, they could take up the pen, or they could move out of their class and its accustomed standards of living. Mary Wollstonecraft provides an example of one such daughter, and she became successively, a governess, a teacher, and a writer, before she became an (independent) wife.[47]

The preponderance of women among eighteenth-century novelists, combined with the low status of this 'literary trade', suggests that at this period of the novel's first expansion, novel-writing might have become a feminized occupation, with all the characteristics of such occupations — low pay and low status. Certainly the commoditization of literature seems to have provided unprecedented opportunities for the entry of women into literary production. But this feminization of fiction was resisted. Men were never less than a substantial minority of its producers, possibly around one third.[48] As fiction proved popular and profitable, and as it won its literary credentials, so men moved back into a position of numerical dominance. By the 1840s the proportion of women producers of fiction had been reduced to about 20 per cent.[49] Did men turn increasingly to fiction because it had become respectable from a literary point of view, or did it become respectable because it had ceased to be a feminine form? Either way we may hazard a confident guess that the participation of men was a necessary condition of the genre being taken seriously as literature. But as men had resisted its feminization in the eighteenth century, so women succeeded in resisting its subsequent masculinization. The figure of 20 per cent is actually high, and marks the novel in particular and the writing of literature in general with a distinct gender-ambiguity which it has never lost.

If women recruited to the production of novels were channelled into this occupation because they did not qualify for more traditional intellectual roles, then they were unlikely to develop that unproblematic and transparent relationship to capitalism and to the bourgeoisie that Gramsci attributed to capitalism's organic intellectuals. The stance which might perhaps come more naturally to such recruits is precisely that which the English novel developed as it achieved literary respectability: a moral, measured and critical distance from capitalism. The manner in which the novel developed, the ideological space it came to occupy, as well as the material conditions of its production and distribution, made it a form more congenial to the daughters of the lesser gentry and the professions. Had the literary response to the commoditization of literature been a romantic bohemianism dedicated to shocking the bourgeoisie, women would have been as effectively excluded as they had been from the ranks of traditional intellectuals. The bohemian is male. *La Bohème* was not an intellectual.

But while the novel's development and institutionalization in nineteenth-century Britain provided a congenial space for women, yet the role of the literary producer was not an easy one to negotiate. Feminist literary theory has analysed and recorded this problematic task faced by women writers, and the strategies they developed for its negotiation. Mary Poovey finds a characteristic 'indirection' in women's writing whose source she locates in the contradictions of feminine propriety. Her analysis of the fiction of Wollstonecraft, Shelley and Austen in relation to the situation of 'the proper lady' throws light on the manner in which women, in their writing, both evaded some of the constraints imposed upon them, yet paradoxically reaffirmed the femininity which defined those constraints.[50] They occupied an ambivalent position viz a viz the way in which the self-identity of the bourgeoisie became bound up with feminine propriety.

Conclusion

Perhaps the major problem of Watt's thesis lies in his attempt to integrate literary and sociological criteria in his definition of the novel. His criteria of selection for novels and novelists for close critical scrutiny are clearly literary, yet his explanatory frame is essentially sociological. He never confronts the possibility of any conflict between the two. Watt has been roundly criticized by Dale Spender for his exclusive concern with the 'founding fathers'. She has restored to the form its early maternal heritage. Watt might reply it was, as a matter of fact, these men who defined the form in *literary* terms, and not the women writers who constituted the majority of its producers. And the conspiracy theory advanced by Spender bears certain difficulties of its own. Yet equally it carries a certain element of truth, and no doubt some interesting women writers will be uncovered in the next few years, under the impact of this re-scrutiny of the novel's early history.[51] Watt was unforgivably cavalier in his automatic dismissal of the majority of women writers, his exclusive attention to the men. But where he is even more exposed to criticism is with respect to the essential sociological component of his definition of the novel. This should have led him to consider not merely those who have been filtered through the lense of critical judgement, but also those who were most influential, and most characteristic at the time: that is to say, women. His *literary* criterion of value is certainly open to question for its sexist bias. But his *sociological* criteria should have compelled him to pay attention to the women writers whom he ignores. The reason for his failure to do so may be sought in the fact that the sociological tradition to which he turned for his understanding of capitalism and its major class, the bourgeoisie, was, like the literary history he utilized, equally obsessed with the male of the species. A consideration of women as members of the bourgeoisie and as writers, would have forced a reassessment not only of the literary critical standards of 'the great tradition' but also the whole definition of the bourgeoisie in terms of male labour and male protestant rationality.

Yet finally Watt is surely right. For the primary parenting of the novel was performed neither by its literary mothers nor its founding fathers, but by capitalism, which both mothered and fathered the new form. This is the kernal of Watt's thesis, and so far it remains unchallenged.

3.

The Novel as Commodity:
1770–1820

Ian Watt, then, identified two interconnected determinants of the emergence of the novel in eighteenth-century Britain, and of the form which it took: the sensibility of the new class of capitalism, the bourgeoisie, and the changed conditions of literary production attendant on the shift from patronage to the market. For Watt, these two determinations converged to produce the same effect, the novel of formal realism. But in his characterization of the early novel Watt took for granted the constraint which producers of commodity fiction were under to create entertaining stories. Where Watt's novel of formal realism is ostensibly governed by commitment to truth and authenticity, it is equally governed by the dictates of imaginative entertainment. The commodity sold in the novel is first and foremost a story which engages the reader's interest and attention.

Watt assumed that the only kind of story which was capable of commanding the interest of the new class was one in which plot, character development and action obeyed the same rules of probability and plausibility which the bourgeoisie believed to obtain in the real social world. They would be entertained by stories about people, places and events in which they could recognize themselves and their world. And so they were. But this was not the only kind of literature which appealed to the bourgeoisie.

The period immediately following the novel's inception saw a great proliferation of the form, and also witnessed a shift away from formal realism towards forms of fiction which registered more clearly its relationship to fantasy and the imagination. Commodities are produced in order to sell. A condition of their continued production is that they sell in sufficient quantities to produce profits — in this case, a return to the publisher on his investment, and to the author, payment adequate to reproduce her labour power. The law of the market lays upon merchandise the necessity to please, if not strictly speaking to be useful. When literature became a commodity and where, as in this period, it openly acknowledged its status as such, it tended not towards that sober realism whose chief aim and object is 'to show things as they really are', but towards non-realist forms often labelled escapist. In other words, the two sets of determinations identified by Watt in bourgeois consciousness and in the capitalist penetration of the literary market, do not necessarily converge to produce a single unified form of fiction. They may pull in opposite directions, and where they do converge to produce the same effect, then this is something that requires explanation. The realist impulse in the novel was given full expression only where it fell under the canon of literature. But as commodity, it fell also under quite different laws.

Gothic fiction has been marginalized by the reconstructed great tradition, so that only a small number of gothic writers are given honourable mention and a minor place in the literary history books. Yet it was an important and popular early bourgeois form, and as such, Watt simply could not afford to overlook it as he did.

Gothic is often discussed in terms of popular fiction rather than bourgeois literature, and is assessed for the contributions it made from the periphery to the centre, the great realist tradition, rather than in its own right. As a popular form, it is usually assimilated to later fictions popular with the working class which it greatly influenced. Yet as David Punter points out, it was not truly popular in the sense in which this term is used today.[1] Like the novels of formal realism analysed by Watt, gothic fiction was written for a bourgeois readership by authors from a similar social background to the producers of realist fiction. If the novel of formal realism was written for and by the bourgeoisie, then so too was gothic fiction which succeeded it to become the dominant form for a while.

The Reading Public and Commodity Fiction

Throughout the eighteenth century and well into the nineteenth the market for the sale of novels was small. Altick estimates that the average print run of a first edition was about 500. 'Only when an author's star was in the ascendant did a publisher venture to order 2000 copies in a first edition, as was the case with Fanny Burney's *Cecilia*.'[2] If we include only those readers who purchased novels, the market was small, and could not have supported the rapid expansion of novel-production which occurred in the last quarter of the century. The potential market was of limited extent in any case. Leaving aside the restrictions imposed by cost, others included the level of literacy, lack of leisure, and of adequate lighting in homes. Altick estimates that in 1780 the national literacy rate was scarcely higher than it had been in Elizabethan times.[3] Watt refers to the novel as 'easy reading' appropriate to the skills of the semi-literate. Students today, faced with *Clarissa* or *Mysteries of Udolpho* may raise their eyebrows at this judgement. Punter is surely nearer the mark in his recognition that very considerable demands were made upon readers even by gothic fiction. These novels were not written in a popular style, but appealed to the same middle-class readers of the novel of formal realism.

The price of novels was high, rising to astronomical proportions after 1790, and peaking with Scott's *Kenilworth*, which sold in 1821 at ten shillings and sixpence per volume, thirty-one and sixpence for the full three volumes; a price and format which were to remain standard until almost the end of the nineteenth century. But in the last quarter of the eighteenth century it would not have been possible to produce novels profitably on a different strategy of high turnover at low unit cost. A mass market for the novel simply did not exist.

It is difficult to be more than speculative here, since demand does not exist in independence of the goods which supply it. Neither is the level of literacy an absolute or given boundary within which the demand for literature is constrained. The lack of reading materials which might have appealed to the working class offered little incentive for the acquisition of reading skills, nor to their exercise once acquired with sufficient frequency to ensure their retention. The level of literacy was itself affected by the supply of reading matter of a kind that might have stimulated the growth of effective literacy, and this dynamic did not get underway until the period of the second expansion of the novel from 1840 onwards.[4] In any case restrictions on time imposed by brutally long working hours, and the appalling condition of working-class housing must also have weighed against the emergence of an extensive working-class readership. As the demand for literature grew among the working class during the course of the nineteenth century it was met first by the notorious penny dreadfuls.[5] The supply of the working-class market tended to be segregated from the start. Novel production was differentiated along lines of class in a marked fashion.

The reading public for novels in the last quarter of the eighteenth century and the beginning of the nineteenth was a small middle-class one, whose boundaries were found among the more prosperous artisans and tradespeople. But this reading public was very much larger than the novel-purchasing public. Novels were, and remained for some time, a rather odd type of commodity. Commodities vary greatly in the length of their useful life. At one extreme they include perishables which must be consumed immediately upon purchase if their use-value to the purchaser is to be realized. At the other extreme, such status-conferring goods as precious jewels retain their use-value almost indefinitely and can be used again and again.

Novels in the eighteenth and early nineteenth centuries were paradoxical commodities in that their usefulness was incommensurate with their durability and their cost. Novels then, as now, are in the main read only once. Novel-readers in the last quarter of the eighteenth century did not wish to be novel-owners. A novel was not considered to be an appropriate addition to the private book collection in the bourgeois home. Even as late as the middle of the nineteenth century, Dickens was looked at askance by George Henry Lewes because his library contained little else besides fiction.[6] With few exceptions such as novels by Fielding and Richardson, they had no ongoing use-value as status-conferring objects once they had been read, and their immediate use-value as entertainment extracted. They could not confer status because of their low repute, unlike the moral, religious and educational works which did find a place on the shelves, and which read or unread, spoke for the class and the cultural pretensions of their owners. Possession of the latest fiction was more likely to be a source of embarrassment than pride. Novels in the last quarter of the century were something to be hidden away, and read in private rather furtively. They were not objects for display in the public parts of the bourgeois home.

'A Byword for Sensationalism' — Minerva Press and Others

The middle class at the time supplied novel-readers, then, rather than novel-purchasers, and this not merely because of the high price at which they were sold, but because they were commodities which were for consumption not possession. For this reason the cover-price of the novel is misleadingly identified as one of the major barriers to the spread of the novel-reading habit. Demand was inelastic relative to price. If the novel had been produced very much more cheaply than it was, it might not have found many more purchasers. In fact a reduction in price of a product already condemned in metaphor as cheap, might have paradoxically had the opposite effect, and delayed the acceptance of the form among the middle class who supplied the bulk of its readership.

A market this small could only be profitably supplied on the basis of low turnover of individual titles at high unit cost, with expansion taking the form of an increase in the number of individual titles, rather than longer print-runs. The key development which made this possible was of course the commercial circulating library. It was the libraries rather than individuals who purchased the novels. Novel-readers wished to read not to own, and the circulating library made it possible to maximize reading without the unwanted embarrassment, cost and inconvenience of permanent acquisition. Because the circulating library supplied a secure and growing demand for reading matter, and because it could make a profit from the loan of books even when the purchase-price was high, the strategy of small print runs at high unit cost was one which satisfied the needs of all parties. Indeed it became evident in the era of Mudie's a little later, when the novel had grown respectable, that it was in the interests of the libraries to keep the cover-price at an artificially high price which positively discouraged private purchase.

Commercial circulating libraries which had begun to appear in the 1720s in London and the fashionable resorts, assumed a key position in the economy of the novel from about 1770 onwards.[7]

The expansion of novel-writing and -reading depended on the expansion of the commercial libraries and vice-versa. They did not make novel-reading cheap. Subscriptions were high. In 1798, William Lane's Minerva Library charged between one and three guineas per annum, depending on the class of subscription. Alternatively the borrower might deposit the face value of the book borrowed, and pay a small fee. Such charges would have placed library subscriptions beyond the means of most working-class families. Novel-reading remained a middle-class pursuit even under the auspices of the libraries. But the library did secure financial viability for an under-capitalized industry, facilitating its expansion to meet the almost insatiable demand for new fiction among this small but growing clientele.

The commercial circulating library dealing primarily in fiction did nothing to enhance the reputation of the novel in the days before Mudie's became a byword for middle-class respectability. The moral panic triggered by the spread of novel-reading in the last quarter of the eighteenth century was indissolubly linked with the circulating library. They shared the same opprobrium which they mutually reinforced. William Lane's Minerva Press and library became synonymous with cheap and nasty fiction. '"Minerva" . . . was a byword for sensational and violently sentiment novels.'[8] The reputation of the early commercial libraries was not helped by some of the sharp practices by which publishers like Lane eked out their profits. Remaindered books were reissued with new titles and title-pages, and plagiarism or near-plagiarisms were commonplace.[9] But even an entrepreneur like the upright Charles Mudie could not have built a prosperous and reputable business out of the circulation of fiction as he was to do some decades later at a point in time when the novel had yet to become a respectable literary form. The libraries were attacked not so much because of the dubious practices in which they sometimes engaged, as because their existence facilitated the production and proliferation of a product widely held to be pernicious and dangerous.[10] Novel-reading was condemned by those intellectual and moral entrepreneurs who had most strongly internalized the 'protestant ethic', in spite of the fact that the pioneers of the book trade were living embodiments of the 'spirit of capitalism' and were usually protestant to boot. William Lane, James Lackington and John Bell, might indeed be considered to be among the ranks of the organic intellectuals of

capitalism. They were among the earliest commercial entrepreneurs of capitalist literary production. James Lackington was
the son of a journeyman shoemaker. He set up in business in
London in 1774 on borrowed capital, and dealt in cut-price books
acquired at auction, chiefly remaindered stock. In 1791 and 1792,
his memoirs claim, he made profits of £4,000 and £5,000
respectively.[11] William Lane followed his father's occupation as
poulterer, a fact which his detractors never allowed him to forget. The commodity switch from birds to books was evidently a
most profitable one, for when he died in 1814, his estate was
valued at about £17,500.[12]

Lane's Minerva Press, which traded under that name from
1790-1820, specialized in the publication of gothic fiction. None
of the gothic writers whose work survives to be read today
appeared under the Minerva imprint, but at the time Minerva
published the most successful authors of the day. Blakey
included a list of the ten best-sellers of 1798 in her book on the
Minerva Press, and noted that all ten were written by women,
though most are now completely unknown. Of Agnes Maria
Bennett's *Vicissitudes Abroad, or the Ghost of my Father* she wrote:
'So high did she stand in her readers' favour that two thousand
copies were sold on the day of publication (1806) though the
price was thirty-six shillings the set.'[13] When Bennett died in
1808 'the whole body of her work ranked her, in the eyes of her
contemporaries at least, with Fielding and Richardson'.[14] Regina
Maria Roche's *Children of the Abbey*, published in 1796, was
immensely popular. It ran through more than eleven editions
and was in print for decades.

Opposition to the Novel

The enormous contemporary success of these writers did not
guarantee them a place in the history books, however, for the
histories were used to construct 'literature' — a status by no
means guaranteed by selling-power. The consensus among those
who have written and rewritten these histories has been that this
first period of expansion of the novel was marked by stagnation
or even retreat, looked at in terms of the development of the
literary potential of the form. J.M.S. Tompkins, who has written
the standard work on the popular fiction of the last quarter of the

eighteenth century, characterizes the novel throughout this period as almost unrelievedly second-rate. The vast majority of novels she assesses as inferior imitations of the examplars left by Richardson, Fielding, Sterne and Smollet. She cites contemporary critics who judged the novel and found it ephemeral, flimsy and disreputable.[15] Taylor documents very fully the widespread opposition to the novel as a cheap and harmful commodity. Both writers stress the importance of women as writers and readers, and link the alleged degeneration of the novel to its feminization. Tompkins reserves her most severe censure for the female novelists of the period. She charges women writers with having 'conspired with the failure in the succession of male novelists of power and seriousness to push back the novel from the position which Fielding had claimed for it and to debase it into a form of female recreation'.[16] The male line having failed to produce legitimate heirs, the heritage passed through the female line and lost its potency: a cautionary tale with a vengeance! This singling out of female writers and of genres popular with women for special scorn is characteristic of studies of popular forms, and mars the work of Dalzeil and James. It is still with us today. Until it began to be studied by feminists, soap opera was dismissed even by writers who were particularly interested in popular television.[17]

Contemporary critics, as we have seen, linked the general shoddiness as they judged it, of the novel not only to the female reader/writer, but also to the novel's commercial status: a commodity catering to 'infantile' female taste. Tompkins, implicitly endorsing this judgement, links this falling away of the novel from the high standards achieved by its 'founding fathers', to a shift away from the preferred critical standards of the period, those of 'moral realism'. The contemporary critic called for and lamented the failure to find, 'invention, instruction (though not too blatantly), well-supported character, and "probability"'.[18] What the critic found instead was sensationalism, sentimentality, fantasy and escapism.

Tompkins, Dalzeil, Altick, James and Watt all write from a perspective thoroughly permeated by the critical standards of the great tradition. They assessed the early novel in terms of this retrospectively known destination towards which the novel was heading. Inevitably perhaps when this great tradition itself came under interrogation from Marxist as well as from feminist perspectives, the reassessments which were made often simply reversed the standards of the canon. The great tradition was reconceptualized under the head of 'bourgeois' or 'classic realism', whose ideological functions were foregrounded in place of its literary credentials. And those forms which produced moral panics, or which were marginalized in the construction of the great tradition, were reappraised for their capacity to disturb, even subvert.

Gothic Fantasy: a Literature of Subversion?

The Literature of Terror as the Underside of Bourgeois Rationality

'... if it should be the case that, as we have suggested, the Gothic novel was fundamentally a middle-class art-form in its origins, we have to ask why it should be the case ... that a class ... should want to turn to a literature which has, to say the least, a deeply ambiguous attitude to the values and practices which that class held most dear'.[19]

Punter's study of the literature of terror concentrates on gothic fiction. In an attempt to explain this early break away from formal realism while at the same time leaving Watt's thesis intact, Punter argues that gothic is the repressed underside of bourgeoise consciousness, a product of excessive reliance on reason and positive science, and the eighteenth-century refusal to recognize the irrational. Quoting Horkheimer and Adorno for support, he argues that irrational fear of the kind that so pervasively informs gothic fiction is both the root and the product of the attempt to bring all things under rational control: '... rationalism will be a self-defeating system, because that which cannot be assimilated will therefore become all the more taboo: reason will create its own enemies'.[20] On Punter's view, realism occupies the middle ground of bourgeois culture, while gothic is its repressed irrationalities displaced onto the margins of that culture. Punter also describes gothic in terms of the young Marx's concept of alienation; a product of the disruption of the social order attendant upon the emergence of industrial capitalism.

The strength of Punter's work lies in his insistence that gothic

is a bourgeois form. He weakens this however by his introduction of the idea that it was a literature of alienation, since
alienation is a condition that rests centrally upon the form of
alienated labour peculiar to capitalism. Why should the conditions of production in the new factories generate a literature of
alienation, when that literature was produced for and by not the
alienated labourers, but the bourgeoisie? The question is the
more puzzling when placed alongside Punter's own recognition
that women, as readers and writers, were so important to this
literary development which appeared at the same time that bourgeois women were being withdrawn from the labour force and
confined to the home.

Punter's study covers a longer time-span than Watt's since he
traces the literature of terror through to the end of the nineteenth
century and into the twentieth. But both writers suffer from a
certain lack of historical specificity. Any thesis which seeks
homologies between aspects of bourgeois consciousness and
developments within fiction necessarily paints a broad canvas,
since the bourgeoisie has been with us for a long time. In the late
eighteenth and early nineteenth centuries it was a class in formation, with fluid boundaries and it generated a broad range of
politics and consciousness, from radicalism to reactionary conservatism. Punter advances on Watt in recognizing the contradictory nature of bourgeois consciousness and in not attempting
to pin it onto a single templet based on Weber's figure of the
protestant producer. But it is still too static and a-historical.

Jacobins and Anti-Jacobins

Marilyn Butler's work on the literature of this period attempts to
locate gothic and other contemporary genres such as sentimentalism in a more precise historical context.[21] She recognizes
the complexity of the task of relating imaginative literature to
political effects in her work on the jacobin and anti-jacobin novel
of the 1790s. She examines the reaction of both to the elevation
of strong feeling so characteristic of the culture of this period, as
seen in the novel of sentiment which had come to prominence
from about 1760.

The overtly political jacobin novelists — Godwin, Bage,
Wollstonecraft — were as hostile to sentimentalism as were their
opponents. The anti-jacobins viewed sentimentalism with deep

suspicion as tending towards moral relativism and individualism, a view Butler regards as not unreasonable: 'The liberal or sentimental tendency is indeed to work against the exercise of the ethical sense, and actively to enlist the reader by half-conscious and almost subliminal means, in the party of tolerance.'[22] She argues that the anti-jacobins were in this respect more perceptive than the jacobin writers they opposed. The jacobin belief in the essential goodness of human nature, and the perfectability of wo/man under the rule of reason lay behind their distrust of any undue indulgence of the emotions. Butler comments: 'It was logical enough for the conservative moralists to preach suspicion of the passions and too close an interest in private experience for its own sake. It was less appropriate for the jacobin: his flight from the irrational represents more of an intellectual failure, just as his unwillingness to depict the inner life as a whole, naturalistically, is retrograde in terms of his form. ... They end by creating central characters with less inward life than the sentimental heroes and heroines whose passivity gives them such offence.'[23]

The tradition of sentimentalism, as well as that of gothic fantasy, was unlike the jacobin novel in that it was not self-consciously political. It was reconstructed in political terms after the event, in the moment of reaction to the French Revolution which saw the birth of modern conservatism: 'Alarmists ... detected subversion in an entire range of fashions acceptable in the 1780s from the cult of tears to the folk ballad, from criticism of lords, clergymen, lawyers, fathers, to the praise of widows, asses and needy knife-grinders.'[24] Butler argues that at the time, late eighteenth-century sentimentalism represented no more than a liberal vein of 'social criticism which informs the work of creative writers of all shades of political opinion'.[25]

For Butler, then, the most characteristic and the most popular forms of this period, the novel of sentiment and the gothic romance, were unselfconsciously and mildly progressive for their cult of individuality and for their sympathetic identification with the victims of tyranny. The villains of this type of fiction are almost uniformly drawn from the ranks of legitimate social authority — 'fathers, father-substitutes, barons, judges, proud men representing authority'[26] and abusing it.

The Fantastic, the Uncanny and the Marvellous

But more radical claims have been advanced for the subversiveness of this fiction, particularly for gothic, on grounds which lie at the level of structure rather than theme. One of the most influential theorists in this reclamation of the popular for subversion is the formalist Tzvetan Todorov.[27] He developed his theory of literature through the analysis of the fantastic, which he defined in terms of its similarity to and difference from adjacent genres. 'The fantastic is that hesitation experienced by a person who knows only the laws of nature, confronting an apparently supernatural event.'[28] It is the imputed reader who hesitates, often along with a character with whom the reader identifies and who also hesitates over the nature of the strange and disturbing events of the narrative. They may after all be explicable in terms of natural causality. They may be the result of delusion, tricks, errors of perception, dreams, madness. Or they may turn out to have been the result of supernatural agencies, or of an unnatural and unknown type of causality. When this hesitation is resolved one way or another in the course of the narrative's progression, the fantastic becomes either the fantastic-uncanny or the fantastic-marvellous, depending on whether natural or supernatural agencies are proved to have been at work. In some instances however the hesitation is never resolved. At the close of the narrative we still cannot be sure. This variant Todorov calls the pure-fantastic, and it is on this type that he bases his claim for the subversive potential of the form.

All three genres, the pure-fantastic, the fantastic-uncanny and the fantastic-marvellous, share certain common features. They are often told in the first person by a narrator who is also centrally concerned in the events narrated. The narrative is frequently set in motion by an uncanny event, something which disturbs normal expectations and which on the face of it is difficult or impossible to explain within known laws. Ann Radcliffe's *Mysteries of Udolpho* might be classed as an instance of the fantastic-uncanny, since the strange happenings which strike horror and terror into the soul of the persecuted heroine Emily, are all given naturalistic explanations. Whereas Matthew Lewis's *The Monk* reveals as the narrative progresses that events which seemed at first sight attributable to mere human evil, are in fact the result of diabolical forces. Here the fantastic is resolved into the fantastic-marvellous.

Mary Shelley's *Frankenstein* may be used to illustrate Todorov's most interesting category, the pure-fantastic. It is told in the first person by a series of narrators whose reliability is open to doubt. The 'I' of narration shifts successively between Robert Walton, a young explorer on a dangerous voyage of discovery to the North Pole, Frankenstein, and the monster he creates. The unnamed monster's narration is at the heart of the novel. But these second two narrators are not independent of the first. The narrative is generated by Walton's letters to his sister Margaret, and later, when he can no longer transmit letters, through his diary. Although both Frankenstein's and the monster's narratives are reported verbatim in the first person by Walton, 'as told to him', Frankenstein's story is relayed through Walton, and the monster's is doubly mediated, by Frankenstein and then by Walton. The reader is not in a position to doubt Frankenstein's reliability as narrator, however implausible his tale, and in spite of its dream-like quality. For it is given partial corroboration at least by Walton, who reports his first sighting of the monster before the appearance of Frankenstein, and who sees the monster at close hand in his cabin at the close of the narrative, when Frankenstein is dead. It is clear that the structure of this complex narrative requires that the narrator whose reliability must be trusted is not Frankenstein, but Walton, and we are given innumerable grounds for hesitation. Walton is remarkably like the man he rescues from the icy water and whose tale he reports. Frankenstein is Walton's alter-ego. Both men are species of over-reachers who have sought forbidden knowledge, assuming the function of the creator. Both have intense relationships with women who stand towards them as sisters; in Walton's case, a full sister, in Frankenstein's, an adopted one whom he is therefore free to marry, but who is a victim of the monster's revenge on her wedding night. Shortly before he meets up with Frankenstein, Walton has written to Margaret of his loneliness, and his longing for a friend, when that ideal friend implausibly appears on a frail and disintegrating vessel in the middle of the ice-floe. And finally, Walton has at this point in the narrative suffered prolonged and severe mental and physical deprivation in his ordeal by water and ice.

The narrative lacks, it is true, any character who can stand in for the imputed reader and give expression within the fiction itself to the reader's hesitation. But Frankenstein himself performs this function to some extent. Even while telling his tale, he draws attention to its implausibility, and at times expresses disbelief. The tale he tells has the logic and the form of a nightmare. Space, time, and probability are defied, as the monster, who seems to grow in stature as the tale progresses, is able to move unseen from one part of Europe to another, and to anticipate his creator's every move. By the time the narrative reaches Scotland and the attempt to create a bride for the monster, the logic of naturalistic cause-effect is almost entirely abandoned (where on this fringe of human society would Frankenstein find the charnal-houses which provided the raw materials for his first creation?) in favour of the logic of paranoia. Frankenstein himself makes several references to the dream-like nature of his experience: 'The whole series of my life appeared to me as a dream; I sometimes doubted if indeed it were all true, for it never presented itself to my mind with the force of reality.'[29] 'During the day I was sustained and inspirited by the hope of night: for in sleep I saw my friends, my wife, and my beloved country. ... Often, when wearied by a toilsome march, I persuaded myself that I was dreaming until night should come and that I should then enjoy reality in the arms of my dearest friends.'[30]

The relationship between Frankenstein and his monster is frequently perceived to be one of dual or split identity. But if the monster is Frankenstein's other self, objectified and persecuting, then the reader must infer that it is Walton who has imagined them both. The reader cannot be certain whether *Frankenstein* is a marvellous tale governed by a causality outside present scientific knowledge — an instance of the 'scientific-marvellous' — or a tale spun out of paranoid delusion and severe sense-deprivation.

For Todorov the fantastic is a radically subversive genre because it crosses and blurs all boundaries and limits. It creates a world in which all kinds of transformations may occur — where self melts into other, subjective into objective. It transgresses the boundaries of the law, and permits the expression of the unmentionable, the forbidden, the shocking. '... incest, homosexuality, love for several persons at once, necrophilia, excessive sensuality ... it is as if we were reading a list of forbidden themes. ...'[31] The censor who is sidestepped in the fantastic is both the institutionalized censor in the public, social world and the internalized, private censor of the individual unconscious.

But more fundamentally, for Todorov, the fantastic transgresses the laws of ordered discourse itself, exposing as it does so the nature of literature and language. It explores and questions the boundaries between fiction and reality: '... today we can no longer believe in an immutable external reality, nor in a literature which is merely the transcription of such a reality. Words have gained an autonomy which things have lost. The literature which has always asserted this other vision is doubtless one of the agencies of such a development.'[32]

Fantasy, Transgression, Subversion

Rosemary Jackson[33] draws heavily on Todorov's model of the fantastic for her study of fantasy, but also on a long line of European theorists. She attempts to rectify the formalist failure or refusal to place literary form in a historical context. She argues for the radically subversive potential of fiction which draws upon the fantastic, and attempts to develop a subversive canon on the underside, so to speak, of the great tradition. Her pantheon is constituted by those authors who have pushed the fantastic along this path of subversion. For she recognizes that it can be developed to quite other ends. The villains are those authors who have opened up the disturbing world of the imagination only in order to re-cover it for bourgeois ideology 'in transcendental rather than transgressive terms'.[34] Here Jackson implicates that tradition of fantasy which takes it into the marvellous, creating self-contained fictional worlds that are quite other than the one with which we are familiar, and which therefore do not engage with or threaten it. This strand of fantasy is involved in the '... creation of secondary worlds, through religious myth, faery, science fiction ... which are *compensatory*.'[35] She includes under this head that type of gothic fiction which engaged in vicarious wish-fulfilment (Ann Radcliffe's for example), and contemporary myth makers such as Tolkien and C.S. Lewis.

A second order of villains is those writers who open up their fiction onto the fantastic and its fears, only to use it as a warning against any temptation to depart from the daylight world of rational conformity: 'A tradition of humanism ... dismisses the demonic as "evil, odious, blatant, vulgar", reading all otherness as mere barbarism, thus reinforcing solid boundaries against the "fantastic" and "unreal".'[36] Under this head are indicted, not surprisingly, writers within the great tradition in their occasional forays into the fantastic — George Eliot, Henry James and Joseph Conrad are singled out.

The counter-pantheon of those who kept faith with the subversive essence of the fantastic consists of those writers whose fiction faces towards both the 'real' and the 'unreal', confronting the former with the latter. They maintain the reader's hesitation until the end. Jackson, like Todorov, finds the 'pure-fantastic' to be its most radical form: 'Like the grotesque, with which it overlaps, the fantastic can be seen as an art of estrangement, resisting closure, opening structures which categorise experience in the name of a "human reality". By drawing attention to the relative nature of these categories the fantastic moves towards a dismantling of the "real", most particularly of the concept of "character" and its ideological assumptions, mocking and parodying a blind faith in psychological coherence and in the value of sublimation as a "civilising" activity.'[37] The heroes and heroines of this counter-pantheon include Sade, Godwin, Mary Shelley, Maturin, James Hogg, Gaskell in some of the stories she wrote for *Household Words*, Dickens, Emily Brontë, Dostoevsky, and more recently, Kafka, Peake and Pynchon.

Jackson, like others of this school, draws on Freud and Lacan in her account of the subversion at work in these texts. They are a collective and public 'return of the repressed'. They make visible, obscurely, what it is in the interests of the dominant culture and a coherent ego to keep hidden. Jackson attempts to give this account a historical dimension by tracing within the literature she discusses a broad process of secularization as the 'other' is no longer seen as supernatural, but increasingly as an externalization of the self. She locates the periodic upsurges of the fantastic, from gothic terror to mid-twentieth century forms, with periods of unusually severe cultural repression: 'The emergence of such literature in periods of relative "stability" (the mid-eighteenth century, late nineteenth, mid-twentieth century) points to a direct relation between cultural repression and its generation of oppositional energies which are *expressed* through various forms of fantasy in art.'[38] Unfortunately the opposite thesis is equally plausible, and indeed is sometimes found, that the fantastic is associated with periods of instability and unrest. Butler does not offer such a broad generalization, but she finds early gothic to be the most radical of the fictions she examines, and she associates this with the French revolution and the revolutionary fervour it excited before reaction set in.

Jackson, like Punter, makes little attempt to map the generic differences she detects onto gender differences. Although she is conscious of the work of feminist writers who have argued that women and men stand in different relationships to culture and language, she doesn't develop this aspect of her theory, remaining content to remark in passing that '. . . it is no accident that so many writers of a gothic tradition are women. . . .'[39] Implicit is an endorsement of the belief that the feminine is, as such, inscribed in 'otherness', and finds expression in the same 'hollowed out spaces' in which the fantastic is sheltered. Women, on this view, have a special affinity with marginal forms of writing, with subversion. The same claim is made by Jackson for all of capitalism's 'others': 'The shadow on the edges of bourgeois culture is variously identified as black, mad, primitive, criminal, socially deprived, deviant, crippled, or (when sexually assertive) female.'[40] Yet the classification on which Jackson creates her subversive pantheon is not related by her to any classification of social and cultural 'otherness'. The question 'whose fantasy?' is never raised, as it surely must be when we are invited to include Sade along with Mary Shelley, Brontë with Dickens?

It has been argued above that *Frankenstein,* by virtue of its narrative structure alone, falls into the category of Todorov's 'pure fantastic', and Jackson, too, claims it for her canon of subversion. Yet others have interpreted it as a socially conservative text.[41] Clearly it may be read in very diverse ways. Jackson celebrates *Frankenstein* as a text with a vision 'lacking faith in progress . . . an index of the *loss* registered through the fantastic. . . . Her [Shelley's] writings open an alternative "tradition" of "female gothic". They fantasize a violent attack on the symbolic order . . . subvert *patriarchal* society and the symbolic order of modern culture.'[42]

Myth and Metaphor: Some Feminist and Marxist Interpretations of Frankenstein.

The claims made by Jackson are large ones and the subversion she identifies operates at a very general level. Ellen Moers offers a more specific reading of *Frankenstein* which in some respects fits in with the view that the fantastic lends itself to the expression of that which is unsayable, even unthinkable, within the culture.[43] Moers' interpretation, like much of *Frankenstein* criticism, depends on metaphorical readings of the text. Moers reads *Frankenstein* as a birth-myth, and relates it to the ambivalence which many mothers experience towards their new born infants, and specifically to Mary Shelley's personal experience of birth and death and their intermingling. *Frankenstein* on this reading allowed Mary Shelley to express a maternal repugnance which she could not openly acknowledge. 'And so', she wrote of the book (and the monster) in her introduction to the second revised version in 1830, 'I bid my hideous progeny go forth. I have an affection for it. . . .'[44]

Marilyn Butler is critical of readings of literature which depend on a psychoanalytic understanding of the author.[45] She argues that the work must be related to the readers' rather than the author's hopes and fears and fantasies. Yet the point about such fantasies is that they have their roots in commonplace experiences which are widely shared. They are not private fantasies peculiar to individual authors who create them.

A feminist critic who offers a very different reading of *Frankenstein* is Mary Poovey. Her reading too is a symbolic one, which sees the monster as Mary Shelley's *literary* progeny rather than her physical offspring. But far from registering an incipient feminism discerned by both Jackson and, for very different reasons, Moers, she sees the novel in terms of the struggle engaged in by women writers with the terms of middle-class propriety, defined by 'the proper lady'. For Poovey, *Frankenstein* figures its author's terror at her own audacity in transgressing the norms of feminine decency not only in her scandalous early life but in the very act of putting pen to paper and engaging in literary production. Egotistic creativity, exhibited by both Walton and Frankenstein, threatens domestic life and relations, and only a proper submission to the demands of domesticity can smother this dangerous energy. 'In *Frankenstein*, the monster simply acts out the implicit context of Frankenstein's desire: just as Frankenstein figuratively murders his family, so the monster literally murders Frankenstein's doomed relationships. . . .'[46]

Unlike Moers and Jackson, Poovey registers the narrative structure of the novel and the strategic place occupied by Walton. On Poovey's reading, Walton becomes the novel's conservative hero. For Walton steps back from the brink, turns away from his audacious quest, back to his beloved sister and home. 'Only Walton is still capable of redirecting his involuted ambitions outward in a self-denying love, for he himself has never permitted his desire to escape completely from the regulating influence of social relationships.' 'Walton's letters, as the dominant chain of all the narratives preserve community despite Frankenstein's destructive self-devotion, for they link him and his correspondents (Mrs Saville and the readers) in a relationship that Frankenstein can neither enter nor destroy.'[47]

Poovey's critical analysis pays close attention to the organization of the text and this is its strength. Yet it is more open than Moers' to Butler's objection that it is overly dependent on psychoanalysis of its author. Fear of literary creativity would be less commonplace among the female readers of *Frankenstein* than maternal ambivalence. Finally this reading does little to explain the endurance of *Frankenstein*. The tale of Mary Shelley's 'hideous progeny' has been told over and over, reworked again and again in twentieth-century cinema. And in the re-telling, the complex narrative structure is lost and with it, the key role of Walton. The core of the tale, so far as its appeal has a more or less constant source, lies in the relationship between Frankenstein and the monster. The hesitations licensed by the novel's narrative structure may moreover be simply missed by the reader and this possibility must be taken into account in any interpretation of its meaning for the reader and its ideological effects.

A different symbolic key has been utilized by Franco Moretti in his interpretation of the text.[48] For Moretti nineteenth-century literary monsters are metaphors for the industrial proletariat, while Frankenstein figures the capitalist, terrified by his own creature. The monster has been forged from '. . . the limbs of those — the "poor" — whom the breakdown of feudal relations has forced into brigandage, poverty and death'.[49] When brought to life it inevitably becomes locked into a self-destructive mutuality with its creator from which neither can escape. The life and death struggle of Frankenstein and the monster figures the struggle at the heart of capitalist class relations.

Butler criticizes Moretti on the grounds that the historical timing is wrong.[50] The metaphorical figure belongs culturally to a later point in time. But she does accept his form of historical-

social interpretation in preference to feminist-psychoanalytic
versions, arguing that Shelley, like Wollstonecraft before her,
utilizes a 'masculine discourse' which is significantly different
from that of 'female gothic'.

However the literature of terror in general and *Frankenstein* in
particular does seem to require a reading which acknowledges its
appeal at the level of psychic fantasy. The question arises
whether the socio-historical and psychoanalytic readings are
mutually exclusive alternatives, or whether they may comple-
ment each other. Although Moretti does not attempt any dual
reading of *Frankenstein* on psychological and sociological planes,
he is committed to this double approach. In his chapter on the
literature of terror, he offers such a reading of that other
enduring nineteenth-century figure of terror Count Dracula.
Dracula figures, according to Moretti, at one and the same time
the Victorian bourgeoisie's fear of capitalism itself and especially
of monopoly capitalism, and the regressive fear of its own cannibalistic desires for its mother which the child projects back onto
her.

Morretti's attempt to reconcile these two readings is particularly interesting in relation to Todorov's insistence that the
fantastic works only when the text is read literally.[51] For Moretti
believes that the texts work by transforming fears first into metaphor, and then into literal monsters. He argues that the essential
function of literature under capitalism is to express, and at the
same time, to hide, its unconscious content and in so doing to
reconcile the individual to a social reality seen as inevitable. The
literature of terror performs this function by its transformation of
socially and psychically derived fears into metaphorical figures
which then take on a life of their own, stalking through the
fiction as uncontrollable monsters. 'In Dracula there is monopoly
capital and the fear of the mother: but these meanings are *subordinated* to the literal presence of the murderous count. ...
Marxism and psychoanalysis ... converge in defining the
function of this literature: to take up within itself determinate
fears in order *to present them in a form different from their real one*: to
transform them into *other* fears so that the readers do not have to
face up to what might really frighten them.'[52]

For Moretti, then, the literature of terror is not so much subversive as exorcist. It expresses the most secret fears and forbidden desires of the social order and the psyche, in suitably

disguised form, and then lays them to rest, reconciling the reader to a mundane reality in which such desires cannot be satisfied and also reassuring her/him that they will not be, since they are feared as well as desired. His overlaying of Marxist and psycho-analytic readings is done tentatively, with due recognition of the difficulties. But his work suffers from a failure to consider the question of the sexual identity of reader and author. And secondly, the difference between a bourgeois reader's fear of a working class grown monstrous and this same reader's mixed fear of and desire for the forbidden pleasures of the unconscious. In his analysis of both *Frankenstein* and *Dracula* Moretti assumes a male reader as well as a bourgeois. A grown woman may have experienced as an infant aggressive cannibalistic desires for her mother which she then projected onto the mother. But the fantasy of the *vagina dentata*, in terms of which Moretti discusses the myth of the vampire, is surely one which would have the most powerful resonance in adult life among males? The adult woman's relationship to the female body, be she heterosexual or lesbian, is simply not one in which this fear would figure very powerfully. Due to their different position in the structure of social relationships, the social fears of bourgeois women are less likely to generate the metaphorical figure of the relationship between labour and capital, more likely, rather, their own feared and desired social and sexual relationship to bourgeois men. Moretti's reading of *Frankenstein* runs into the same difficulties which beset Punter's account of gothic as a literature of alien-ation, due to his failure to consider questions of gender as well as class, and of their inter-relationship.

Conclusion

Repression and Subversion in the Novel

Two different kinds of subversion have been elided in the 'fan-tastic as subversion' thesis: subversion of a socially constructed class society in which women are systematically subordinated to men; and subversion of a precarious psychic order which secures a viable personal identity for the individual within that social order. Moretti argues that in literature we indeed witness a 'return of the repressed' but in a form which also affirms the necessity of repression. He contests the assumption that 'the greatest happiness we could find would be to express and live the unconscious contents of the psyche fully and without restraint'.[53] Such an eventuality, were it possible, would rather, he contends, produce the exact opposite of pleasure. Hence the fear which characteristically is inseparable from the forbidden desire. The pleasure of the text lies not in 'the perception of a "return" of the unconscious, but rather in its exact opposite: in the contemplation of a successful compromise'.[54]

The formation of a rational ego prepared to forgo, albeit reluctantly, these dangerous pleasures is not peculiar to any one form of society, although the specific contents of unconscious desires may be variable according to time and place. Presumably then, some kind of compensatory literature will be necessary in any society, including any conceivable socialist-feminist future. The creation of an unconscious is the necessary effect of the creation of a social self, and as long as this is the case, then a literature which both expresses and disguises the content of the unconscious, the desire for acting out, and the desire for repression, will continue to find a readership. When posed in terms of psychoanalytic readings of this type of literature, the question of subversion simply cannot be answered. Such literature is no more and no less subversive in this sense than dreams. If worked upon by the reader in the manner in which the patient and the analyst work upon the patient's dreams, such literature might function to reveal rather than conceal, to transform socially produced neuroses into 'common unhappiness'.[55] But when all is revealed, and the psychodrama beneath the fantasy is exposed, do we not need to go on dreaming? Are we not still frightened by imaginary monsters?

However the second type of repression with which this first is elided, has to do with the expression and disguise/denial of fears and hopes of social transformation and these are not, or are not always, analogous to the fears and desires of the unconscious. Unlike the latter they may be realizable. The fear of the dangerous creature unleashed by capitalism, the industrial proletariat, which may or may not be figured by Mary Shelley's monster, is a determinate fear only for *one* class of capitalism, the bourgeoisie. What the bourgeoisie fears, the working class may have good reason to wish and hope for. Unlike the desires and fears generated in the process of becoming an individual human being, and repressed into the unconscious, the desires and fears generated by the capitalist mode of production are differentially distributed, like the wealth it creates. The ambiguity of the bourgeoisie towards the proletariat is not like the ambiguity of the individual towards repressed unconscious desires. The ambiguity of capitalism may be defined thus: capitalism produces and depends upon that which it exploits and dominates, but also fears. If Frankenstein's monster figures the proletariat for its bourgeois readers, then the metaphor breaks down, as Moretti recognizes, insofar as the monster is of no use to Frankenstein, whereas the bourgeoisie depends for its existence on the production of surplus-value by the proletariat. Capitalism could not kill its monster without destroying itself. Bourgeois dependence on the proletariat however only increased the fear. It was not a fear overlaid by desire, but increased by dependency. It could be tempered only by the hope that the monster might be controlled and contained.

The double-function of the literature of terror when it is viewed psychoanalytically is that of both expressing desire, and allaying the fears which desire simultaneously arouses by reconciling the individual to the impossibility of satisfaction. But the *social* desires and fears expressed in the literature of terror were split. For the fear belonged to one party to the major social relationship of capitalism, the desire to another. The bourgeoisie craved reassurance that what they feared might not happen; the proletariat hoped that what the bourgeoisie feared might be realized. While Moretti's attempt to integrate psychoanalytic and materialist interpretation is an interesting and important one, any such attempt will have to take account of these systematic differences between the two levels of interpretation.

Because Mary Shelley's novel was written for a bourgeois readership, the question of its significance for a working-class readership need not trouble us here. But the fact that it was written by a woman, and read by women as well as men means that the question of its relationship to determinate female fears cannot be evaded.

The working class is socially positioned in subordination to capital and the capitalist, and culturally positioned in inferiority. Bourgeois women, as members of their class, share in class domination and 'superiority', but are positioned as subordinate and inferior to the men of their own class. There are reasons to suppose that the 'naturalness' of patriarchy may be more fully 'lived' by bourgeois women than is the 'naturalness' of class oppression by the working class. Class identity, like sexed identity, is learned in interaction in the family in the first instance. But the class identity which the child learns is one shared by the entire family — a source of common identity and solidarity. This is not true of sexed identity, which divides family members and locks them into rivalries which may be more powerful than same-sex solidarities. A key component of working-class identity has almost always been a solidaristic refusal of this positioning in subordination and inferiority as anything but unfair, unjust, unwarranted. It is true that there is a tradition of working-class deference. But there is also available a powerful culture of refusal and resistance. There is also a counter-culture of feminine refusal. But the promises offered the 'good' woman who conforms are tremendously seductive. Throughout the whole history of white middle-class feminism it has proved extremely difficult to forge a feminist critique which is not implicated in some aspect of conventional femininity and its role. One reason is the way in which class privilege was historically made conditional upon feminine propriety.[56] A second is that women's desires and hopes are developed and channelled through their learning of a problematic feminine identity. Workers may actually have more to lose than Marx thought in uniting against capitalism. Women risked their class identity (which as socialists we might consider well lost) but also the loss of opportunity to pursue personal hopes in which they had made considerable psychic investment. As feminists, we have a tendency to counter the false 'real woman' of ideologies of femininity with a real 'real woman' who is a feminist heroine: 'underneath, we're all feminists'; behind every submissive, feminine woman is an angry, raging feminist struggling to come out. The truth may be rather that of a systematic ambiguity, more or less deeply felt by all women engaged in the business of constructing a sense of self and social identity, whether their persona tends to feminine conformity or feminist rebellion.

Feminism and the Subversive Text

The question I want to return to finally is this. If women have developed their contradictory and ambivalent hopes and fears in a patriarchal order of domination and subordination, and if the condition of realizing these hopes in however truncated a form is submission to that order of domination, one in which their worst fears may also be realized, what in this context would constitute a 'subversive' text? Firstly, it would be a text which will be read. The first imperative of commodity literature is to entertain its readers. The subversive text must give pleasure to a female readership while at the same time disturbing the foundations of that pleasure. The relationship of women to patriarchal domination, is more like the relationship of the individual to unconscious desires, than is the relationship of the working class to capitalism. The bourgeois readers of gothic fantasy desired the rewards of feminine conformity yet simultaneously feared the dangers of submission to male domination. A fiction that gives pleasure in these circumstances will surely be one which expresses this double ambiguity. And on Mary Poovey's analysis, this is exactly what we find in so much fiction written by women and read by them. If Moretti is right in identifying the function of the literature of terror in its ability to both express and deny forbidden desires, then it may well have also served the negotiation of women's contradictory relationship to patriarchal capitalism.

What sense does it make to label such a literature 'subversive' from a feminist point of view? It reproduced the middle-class woman's relationship to patriarchal capitalism. But the relationship it reproduced is a deeply ambivalent one, which protested while it submitted. It may be read as conciliatory, reconciling women to their own subordination. It may also be read as reproducing and reinforcing women's characteristic fears of male domination, their resentment against it, and wish to escape it. Such a literature, like the rituals and ceremonies of precapitalist society, may create as much anxiety and hostility as it allays. It is neither unambiguously subversive, nor unambiguously conciliatory. It was not until it began to seem possible to achieve reforms in gender relations and the position of women that a fiction which could express opposition to the male regime in less disguised fashion began to appear. By this time, the dominant form of bourgeois fiction was one which presented itself as literature rather than as commerce or entertainment in commodity form, and whose prevailing literary convention was that of realism. We shall be examining some of this fiction in chapters 5 and 6. Meanwhile chapter 4 looks at the changes in literary production and consumption as they affected women readers and writers in the second period of expansion of the novel, from 1840 to almost the end of the nineteenth century.

4.

The Novel as Literature: 1840-94

While the capacity of the novel to generate literature had been established by the lasting reputation of its 'founding fathers', its tendency to actually produce 'mere entertainment' was held against it during the first period of its expansion in the last few decades of the eighteenth century. The doubts commonly expressed about the novel centred as we have seen around three of its characteristics; its commercialism, its feminization, and the dominance of non-realist, 'escapist' forms. I have argued that, given the marginal position occupied by the novel at this time within the literary culture, its ability to contribute to the maintenance of bourgeois hegemony through the literary celebration and exploration of the classical bourgeois virtues, or through the interpellation of a bourgeois subject if you will, was slight. From an ideological point of view it is more profitable to examine the early novel in terms of psychic and social fears, hopes, wishes, fantasies which could not be openly acknowledged nor brought fully within the frame of the dominant ideology. Commodity fiction anticipated the contradiction between the virtues celebrated in capitalist production, and the pleasures promised in the capitalist market-place. Moreover the fears and anxieties to which it gave expression may have been allayed in its formal resolutions, but were equally reproduced and kept alive.

In the early decades of the nineteenth century the situation of the novel changed significantly on all three counts. It remained a commodity; but the manner of its production and distribution foregrounded its literary claims, masked its relationship to commerce. Secondly, although women continued to play a major part as consumers of fiction, and a substantial one as producers, the production of quality fiction had by this time become a male-dominated profession. Thirdly, the restoration of the novel's literary credentials was marked by a decided shift back towards the dominance of a realist aesthetic.

By the 1840s, on Tillotson's analysis, the novel had become *the* dominant form of literature in Britain.[1] It is interesting to note the congruence with Escarpit's quantitatively based analysis of French literary production.[2] He shows the novel overtaking poetry and drama in France at roughly the same period of time. The dominance of realism is evidenced by the fact that almost the entire 'great tradition' was written in this period between 1840-94.[3] No terrifying monsters stalk its pages. If real social and psychic fears were expressed and allayed in this literary fiction, they necessarily took a different form.

The literary and class respectability of the novel in this period altered its ideological bearings. It was constrained to address capitalism's more public presentation of itself in a way that fantasy fiction was not: its Sunday face of pious speeches and sober bourgeois virtues. Yet it remained a commodity and, as such, constrained by the need to entertain its readers. In this it was almost unique among the bearers of classical bourgeois ideology. While scholarship, sermons and political writings have certainly furnished profitable business for writers and publishers, they are insulated from the market to some extent by their relationship to powerful institutions which are not funded through the purchase and sale of commodities: the university, the church, the state, political parties. The novel at this stage, prior to the institutionalization of English studies within the education system, had no such insulation. It depended on profitability, but its rationale was its literary value. Insofar as intellectual and literary production took a commodity form, it tended towards the denial and disguise of its own commodity status. The salience of use- and exchange-value had to be reversed from the usual order of precedence in capitalist commodity production. *Adam Bede* might be a gold-mine for its writer and publisher, but this had to be seen as incidental. The motor car may be produced in order to make money without its roadworthiness being impugned. But 'literature' cannot be written in order to make money without undermining its literary status.

Novel Production and Distribution

It was argued in the last chapter that the size of the market for the purchase of novels, given their low status-conferring power in the late eighteenth century, dictated a strategy of small print runs at high unit cost, with expansion taking the form of an increase in the number of titles rather than the number of copies. This strategy depended on the development of the commercial circulating library. This system of production and distribution remained basically unaltered throughout the nineteenth century in spite of the changed status of the novel and the great expansion of the reading public.

The publication of 'quality' fiction was dominated, throughout much of this period, by only seven major publishers: Chapman and Hall, Bradbury and Evans, MacMillans, Longmans, Smith and Elder, Bentleys, and Blackwoods. These were selfconsciously literary publishers, unlike the Minerva Press which had specialized in the production of popular gothic in the earlier period. They published, as Sutherland puts it, '... above the literary threshold'.[4] Between them they published most of the nineteenth-century novels which were later reconstructed as the great tradition.

As capitalist business firms, these publishers were obliged to produce their stock in trade at a profit. But good literature does not necessarily make good business, and there was a conscious tension produced by this double commitment, one which was negotiated in a variety of ways. Arthur Waugh's history of Chapman and Hall opens with a telling sketch of its two founders. Edward Chapman, who '... had always shown a taste for books, and a meditative, studious mind ...' was therefore 'naturally' not a good business man. His partner, William Hall, was needed to supply the secondary but essential business acumen.[5]

As the novel gained in literary status and as the reading-public expanded, production might have been reorganized along the lines on which it developed in America, with long print runs at low unit cost to encourage the buying habit. But the borrowing habit was too well established in the earlier decades, and the arrival on the scene of Mudie's Select Library settled the matter. Production of a large number of titles with small print runs at high unit cost, with access by loan rather than purchase, remained the norm throughout the century. Quality novels were produced in expensive three-decker editions, on good quality paper, with large print, and generous margins. They were sold at a price which almost nobody actually paid: ten shillings and sixpence the volume, thirty-one and sixpence the set. Sutherland has shown that this was a format which was economically viable for both publisher and author. At the bottom end of the market, a novel might earn only £100 for its author, while at the top, George Eliot was paid £7,000 for *Romola* and Disraeli hit the jackpot with £10,000 for *Endymion*, in a transaction which lost money for his publisher. But the system normally secured the publisher a safe if modest return on investment, and the author an equally modest middle-class income.[6]

The library was of course the key institution in this system. The three-decker edition in which literary fiction first appeared was bought almost exclusively by the libraries, although not at the cover price of one and a half guineas. Discounts varied, but the average price paid seems to have been a little less than half of this. The library edition would usually be followed a year or two later by a cheap reprint, once library demand had been satisfied. The price of reprints and cheap railway editions fell over the century, as publishing and printing costs fell and demand rose. But the three-decker first edition remained at the same inflated price throughout. Access to new fiction by readers in the first instance continued to be by loan, with the exception of those novels that first appeared in serial or part publication before coming out in a library edition.

Mudie's Select Library was founded in 1842 by Charles Edward Mudie who was, like his father, a businessman in printing and stationery. His social background was not unlike that of the earlier generation of entrepreneurs in the booktrade discussed in chapter three. He could stand in very well indeed for Weber's figure of the typical protestant capitalist producer. He was Scottish, and a fundamentalist, and his morality was quintessentially 'Victorian': 'No longer would the head of a Victorian family need to waste his time scanning circulating library works to see whether they were suitable for his daughters; no longer would the daughter, like Lydia Languish, have to throw her book behind the sofa at the entrance of her parents. . . .'[7]

The library served a middle-class clientele. This restriction was not a function of cost alone — library subscriptions were remarkably cheap compared to those of the earlier generation of libraries. Mudie's policy of 'selection', and the whole ambience of the building itself, were calculated to appeal to this clientele: '. . . the stuccoed Regency building was, in the Athenaeum's judgement, one of the most successfully designed classic structures in London. At semi-circular counters customers exchanged their books in the great round hall, which was reminiscent "of the British Museum Reading Room on a small scale". . . . The roof was supported by Ionic columns, whose forms were repeated by pilasters on the walls. . . .'[8] Buildings, like books and paintings, address their users and offer an identification of the user and of the activity conducted within its walls. Formally the architecture of Mudie's was not unlike the style adopted later by the great municipal libraries. The typical Carnegie library unites municipal pride with classical splendour. It speaks of the lofty vision and philanthropic largesse of the men whose charities founded it. These libraries were initially aimed at attracting the respectable working class, and their address to these users spoke of self-improvement, rational leisure and sobriety. Neither the public library (understandably, since it was financed out of the product of a penny rate), nor Mudie's, spoke of commerce. Despite Mudie's unfashionable location in New Oxford Street, the library was stamped unmistakably with the insignia of both middle-class respectability and literary pretension.

While there was some considerable overlap of reading publics, so that an author like Dickens could launch his novels in the rival form of serial or part publication, Mudie and the big seven publishers catered by and large to a middle-class readership, while working-class taste was satisfied elsewhere. Sutherland estimates that for each quality publisher '. . . publishing above the literary threshold, there were ten beneath'.[9]

The Production of Literature and the Production of Profits

Capital may be accumulated through the strategy of small-scale production for an exclusive market, in a manner that is personalized, or through production at low unit cost on a large scale which depends on standardization and mass appeal. The transformation of art by commodity production from the eighteenth century onwards created delicate problems of negotiation between these two strategies. For the type of commodity in question, catering as it does to wants which 'spring from the fancy', may derive use-value less from any intrinsic useful properties than from a scarcity which grants status-exclusivity. Mass produced, commodities such as precious jewels, Persian carpets, or foreign travel lose their use-value insofar as this resides in their capacity to confer status-exclusivity — the power to act as markers of money and privilege. The search for unassailable marks of status is unending and ultimately self-defeating under capitalism. Rosalind Williams has traced the process whereby the dandy and aesthete Robert de Montesquiou, the model for Huysmans' des Esseintes, ran rapidly through this logic in which the power of the market and of imitative mass consumption is denied and paradoxically affirmed at the same time.[10] She sees Montesquiou and his type, the dandy, as engaged in an attempt to establish a new aristocracy of taste, in opposition to the democratized market which, when successful, inspires mass imitation which defeats the purpose of the exercise.

The production of commoditized art faced a parallel dilemma. If art and literature are defined in terms which look towards an educated and discerning elite who are seeking aesthetic pleasures rather than entertainment, then popularity becomes problematic. On the one hand capitalist commodity production entails profit maximization which might be assumed to depend on maximum exposure and popularity. On the other hand, if works of art and literature are *too* popular, make too much money, then their aesthetic credentials may be called into question.

Different art forms negotiated this problem in different ways as they entered the era of commodity art. The most valuable art object is the one which is absolutely unique. The original painting is the most obvious paradigm. Its status-value, like its market price, depends on its actually being the original of a work accredited in the right circles as great, and not a copy, however perfect. Benjamin believed that the 'aura' of a work of art was undermined by mechanical reproduction.[11] Yet in some respects it may actually have been enhanced. For mechanical reproduction allows the circulation of copies which familiarize people with pictures which they rarely have the opportunity to see in the original. Aura may be experienced in finally standing before the original, in the knowledge that this is the thing itself, so familiar from the endlessly circulated copies, yet at the same time so different in the flesh. The quality of the reproduction is immaterial to this process of creating aura. The extent to which aesthetic properties of the original are reproduced in the copy varies a great deal, but the poorest copy may *signify* properties it cannot reproduce, and in so doing, enhance the reputation and the aura of the original.

Popularity through mechanical reproduction cannot in itself establish the reputation of a painting and a painter, however. The path that must be followed is determined by the manner of institutionalization of the art world of painting, and is normally through exhibition in museums and galleries. Familiarization among a wider public through the circulation of reproductions is usually a subsequent stage. Reputation must first be established among the cognoscenti.[12]

Novels present quite different problems of negotiation between literary reputation and popularity. Literariness is not lost in reproduction, and so in principle a long print run should not affect literary reputations. But as with painting, to be too popular prematurely may be damaging. Yet the material interests of both author and publisher lie in profit maximization. The price the author can obtain for an MSS and the profit to the publisher depends on the size of readership not on the literary reputation, and the latter is not in any case determined in the court of popular appeal. Insofar as it is, specifically, literature which is being offered for sale, there is a tension between material reward and literary standing. This tension was very apparent among the nineteenth-century authors of the great tradition. It can be seen in George Eliot's equivocal response to the popularity of her novels: 'She was caught between two opposing pressures: the artist's inherent suspicion of popularity, and her own driving need to reach and be favourably accepted by as large a reading audience as possible without prostituting her art. When this latter need was unexpectedly met by *Adam Bede*, which she had written without even a thought of popular success, she felt justified in looking to sales rather than reviews, as a sign of the worth of her writing. She became hawklike in watching the advertising that the Blackwoods did for her works and was always morbidly convinced it was inadequate'.[13]

Redinger offers an explanation for Eliot's hawklike attitude in terms of the psychological insecurities of childhood, but what is interesting is that a special explanation should be sought at all. The reason her biographer felt compelled to look for one is revealing of the strength of the belief, still with us today, that art and literature, being on a higher plane, are above mere material interests, and that the two are, if not incompatible, at least incongruous. Yet there is little evidence to suggest that those who have an interest in the production of work of literary value are or should be adverse to making money out of its production. Dickens, too, never came to terms with the pirating of his work in America, and this hardly requires any psychological explanation. His material interests were at stake.

Blackwood, Eliot's publisher, wrote to a member of his staff after Eliot had sold *Romola* to a rival firm, in restrained disapproval: 'The conduct of our friends in Blandford Square is certainly not pleasing nor in the long run will they find it wise however great the bribe may have been . . .'[14] while George Simpson, Blackwood's printing manager in Edinburgh, referred to Eliot more simply as 'an avaricious soul'.[15] Eliot herself tried to trace and rationalize a narrow moral path between just reward to the author and the irresponsible peddling of wares to the highest bidder, in a rather ponderous essay on authorship which was not published in her lifetime. She argued that the writer who writes only with a view to the market ' . . . carries on authorship on the principle of the gin palace. And bad literature of the sort called amusing is spiritual gin. A writer capable of being popular can only escape this social culpability by first of all getting a profound sense that literature is good-for-nothing if it is not admirably good . . .' but then 'It is in the highest sense lawful for him to get as good a price as he honourably can for the best work he is capable of. . . .'[16] The tone is that of the traditional intellectual, but also of bourgeois virtue confronted by the temptations of the capitalist market-place.

A hundred years later John Fowles's literary reputation was hampered by his success in the best-seller market. Critics hostile to Fowles inevitably use his popularity as evidence of his dubious literary standing, while those who wish to claim him as a great modern writer are conversely almost apologetic about his sales.[17]

The three-decker library system through which the production and distribution of so much of the literary fiction of the nineteenth century was organized functioned in a manner analogous to the gallery/museum system for painting. It allowed the author as well as the publisher and the reader to negotiate the potentially conflicting requirements of the novel as commodity, as literature, and as ideology. It was a system amenable to a high degree of control. There were certain key gate-keeper roles in the system, most notably of course that of the librarian. Others included the readers for the literary publishers. Geraldine Jewsbury, as reader for Bentleys for many years in the second half of the century, had enormous influence in determining what saw the light of day, as did George Meredith in his years as reader for Chapmans from 1860-91. Between them, a small group of men and women were effective arbiters of literary taste in fiction, operating an informal critical and ideological censorship. The standards by which they determined which MSS should pass were a mix of moral, critical and commercial, as may be seen by the reports written by Jewsbury which are collected in the British Museum.[18] But the system did ensure that whatever happened in continental Europe, English authors of literary fiction would not be tempted to engage in the business of shocking the bourgeoisie in the name of literature.

Women and Literary Fiction

If Altick's estimate of the relative numbers of men and women producing literature in the nineteenth century may be relied upon, and unless the proportions were very different in the case of fiction, then women would appear to have suffered a considerable reversal by the time that the novel had achieved literary respectability. The appearance may in fact be misleading.[19]

Although women may have been proportionately less well represented by the 1840s than they had been in the eighteenth century, there were far more of them, in absolute terms, writing novels. Watt estimates that during the eighteenth century a total of about 2000 novels was produced.[20] Showalter puts the figure for Victorian fiction at over 40,000.[21] It must be remembered too, that the figure of 20 per cent, which may underrepresent the proportion of women novelists as opposed to producers of literature of all types, is still very high for a middle-class profession. It would be high even today in a profession which is not feminized. For example, the proportion of women in university teaching in 1979 was only about 13 per cent and this is fairly typical of a whole range of male-dominated professions.[22] Finally, while it is true that women were overtaken by men in terms of the relative numbers of producers of fiction, they improved their position with respect to literary reputation. Dale Spender attributes the absence of women writers from the histories of eighteenth-century literature to a male conspiracy which contrived to distort that history and even to steal women's literary inventions.[23] Yet nineteenth-century histories of literature read differently. Here a number of women feature prominently. Paradoxically, as women produced relatively less, relatively more of them gained lasting literary reputations. But the literary critical establishment was no less male-dominated than it had been in the eighteenth century. Literature was still overwhelmingly policed by men.

Women entered the production of fiction in the Victorian period on different terms than they had in the eighteenth century. One indication of the difference is the often noted gender shift in the adoption of pseudonyms. When the novel was dominated by women, men were as likely to adopt feminine pseudonyms as women were to adopt a masculine name. One reason for this was the predominance of 'woman-to-woman' address in eighteenth-century fiction. The imputed author being female, a feminine authorial name might well be considered appropriate, whatever the actual sex of the author. For similar reasons, men sometimes adopt feminine pseudonyms when writing romantic Mills and Boon-type fiction. The shift in the gender of pseudonyms in the Victorian period may perhaps indicate a change in the prevailing address of fiction. The imputed author of novels which aspired to the title of great literature was a human being. But while Spender's terse injunction 'think male for man'[24] does not always hold, it is a good rule of thumb. Women writers might well have found it expedient to disguise their sex in creating a normatively 'human' author.

We may perhaps generalize here, a little speculatively it is true. In the period up to the end of the eighteenth century or thereabouts, women dominated novel production, and produced primarily woman-to-woman fiction which had a predominantly female readership. By the 1840s and in 'serious' realist fiction, women were writing novels which addressed men as well as women, and the novel-reading public now included a higher proportion of men than had been the case in the earlier period. It was this shift in address that may explain the fact that while women were writing proportionately fewer novels than they had been, proportionately more of them were successful in the long term as literature. A condition of literary canonization, then, may have been not so much that the author must be male, as that the work must be addressed to men and read by them, and not addressed exclusively to women.

But while 'human' is indeed normatively male, nevertheless the great humanist tradition of realist fiction offered a place from which a woman could speak as a woman. Not all authors adopted masculine pseudonyms. Jane Austen wrote, anonymously, it is true — but as 'a lady'. And Elizabeth Gaskell made little attempt to disguise her sex although she, too, preferred anonymity as long as her cover could be maintained.

The nineteenth-century great tradition has been analysed over and over again, and has had its few distinguished women re-scrutinized more recently within feminist criticism. We have now a reputable body of feminist criticism of these authors, and it is not the intention to attempt to add to this here.[25] I will limit myself to a few remarks about Elizabeth Gaskell because she has been relatively neglected in this corpus, and because of the place she came to occupy as a literary producer in terms legitimated within the dominant domestic ideology of the times.

Middle-Class Femininity

Not only has Elizabeth Gaskell received the least attention from feminist criticism,[26] but she also is, among her distinguished sister-writers, the one who seems to have 'lived' most fully, to have appeared most comfortable within the confined space of a conventional middle-class femininity.

Writing of working-class women, Barbara Taylor has insisted that what has come to be known as 'the ideology of domesticity' was not '. . . just a set of oppressive ideas foisted upon a supine female population; it was actively adopted by many working-class women as the best in a narrow range of alternatives'.[27] The point she makes may be generalized. It was an ideology actively chosen and lived, too, by many of the middle-class women who were the first among the new classes of capitalism to come under its dictates. Indeed it must be doubted whether any ideology can become powerful without the active and positive compliance of those governed by it. It is not my intention to endorse Branca's portrait of a 'silent majority' of active, busy and contented housewives throwing themselves wholeheartedly into the new role which they forged for themselves — petty bourgeois heroines of a rewritten drama of 'modernisation'.[28] But Branca is right to insist that middle-class women had a very considerable stake in their ideologically sanctioned role. Mary Poovey makes a similar point with respect to the psychic aspects of that invest-ment when she describes the ideology of domesticity as enabling as well as constraining, and it was this psychic investment that was the primary focus in discussing the literature of terror and fantasy in the last chapter. Poovey argues that '. . . most women probably found a large measure of personal satisfaction in their daily occupations . . . and . . . their desires no doubt did begin to seem — even to themselves — more or less commensurate with their duties', . . . and that '. . . women had a clear investment in accepting the naturalization of the feminine ideal'.[29] This for-mulation allows for the coexistence, in different degrees of balance, of both a commitment and a simultaneous resistance, more or less conscious or repressed, to femininity as it was constructed within that ideology. It all hinges on the 'more or less'. Poovey recognizes the degree of psychic female energy which might remain free-floating and available for less orthodox outlets where these were or became available.

This section will be more concerned with the social aspects of the middle-class investment in domesticated femininity, which was equally substantial. Women had a real material interest in submission to an order which identified them as inferior to the men of their class. The middle-class woman enjoyed material advantages through marriage which could not have been hers had she struck out for independence. Daughters did not inherit wealth, save exceptionally, and only exceptionally might they become capitalists in their own right. The woman who earned her own living would be poor because female earnings were so low, and declassed by virtue of the fact that she worked. Even recognized exceptions such as governessing placed her in the unenviable position of the sociological 'skidder' — on the way down and out. Perhaps the only exception was the woman who earned substantial sums by writing.

While women stand in a different and less secure relationship to their social class than do men, nevertheless their vicarious membership of the bourgeoisie through family relationships to bourgeois males carries with it distinct material interests in defending class and its privileges. It is therefore not surprising that bourgeois women, too, were complicit in the construction and maintenance of a gender order that disadvantaged them, when conformity to that gender order was a condition of their ability to defend class-membership and privileges. At the social level, a form of rational compliance was indicated which would strongly reinforce any investment made already at the psychic level.

However rational compliance does not necessarily entail wholehearted, internalized acquiescence to all aspects of domestic ideology. Dissent might be registered with safety in a wide variety of ways. There was space to register a certain sceptical distance from beliefs and practices which were not openly challenged. One such effective register was offered by comedy. Writing of Fanny Burney, Judy Simons states: 'What we have is the disparity (displayed through so much nineteenth century literature written by women) between the public role and the inner life. The woman is a shrewd and perceptive observer of a male dominated society, and by exposing it, undermines its validity. Simultaneously, however, there is a wry acceptance of the power of this world and women's dependence on it as their only means of survival. Burney provided the key, technically, to irony, the woman's weapon against the male regime. It was from this basis that so many later women writers developed'.[30] In effect comedy allowed women writers to say 'we will go along with such absurdities because we need must, but please don't think that we take them or you altogether seriously'.

Elizabeth Gaskell

Realism versus Melodrama

Elizabeth Gaskell's fiction is almost entirely innocent of irony at the expense of men, or 'the male regime'. Rather her work illustrates another option open to middle-class women and writers in the negotiation of domestic ideology. In her writing she gives the feminine role and identity pivotal importance in the construction and maintenance of social life. This strategy is common in woman-to-woman genres, and Gaskell's novels share some features of these forms. *Mary Barton* finds its place within the great tradition by virtue of its descriptive realism in introducing the author's middle-class readers to the living conditions of the working class. Its central concern is *the* social problem of her time, the 'condition of England' question. But her novel is usually also seen as flawed by a retreat into melodrama. Certainly it has a highly melodramatic plot. It shares what Ien Ang has called 'the tragic view' of today's television soap operas.[31] There are nine deaths, if my tally is correct, in the course of its pages, one of which is murder. Another victim, Aunt Esther, supplies the secondary theme of the fallen woman become prostitute. The narrative is about family relationships as much as it is about the relationship between masters and men, and it offers the familial model as the potential basis for reconstituting the latter on a sound footing.

But the family is the site, above all, of great suffering and great sacrifice on the part of its female members, and it is this which gives the book its resemblance to today's soaps. The women of the family learn to endure and to forbear. They spend much of their time waiting. The heroine alone is offered the opportunity to display her heroism as she initiates the search for Will Wilson which terminates in the exciting chase after his departing vessel in the waters of Liverpool. Her success saves her lover, Jem, from death by hanging for a murder he did not commit. She is even allowed an almost unprecedented privilege in the modest and chaste heroine — that of publicly declaring her love for Jem, which he learns of for the first time as she gives her testimony from the witness box.

Raymond Williams's analysis of *Mary Barton* has coloured most subsequent left interpretations of this novel.[32] He categorizes it as an industrial novel, and locates its best moments in its documentary realism: 'The really impressive thing about the book is the intensity of the effort to record, in its own terms, the feel of everyday life in the working-class homes'.[33] The shift into melodrama he dismisses as '. . . the familiar and orthodox plot of the Victorian novel of sentiment. . . .'[34] He explains this shift in terms of contradictory 'structures of feeling' which inform the novel — on the one hand, sympathy with the suffering of the working class, and on the other, fear of violence. Yet the melodrama is pervasive, and does not depend entirely on the uncharacteristic political murder. The incidents of family suffering are the very stuff of women's melodrama, including many contemporary soaps. But the novel lacks, of course, soap opera's open-ended structure.

Woman-to-Woman: Woman-to-People

A second difference between the two may be located in a difference of address. Today's soaps are predominantly woman-to-woman forms. *Mary Barton* is woman-to-people/men. It addresses men as well as women, and in this case, quite crucially, the former. Gaskell published this her first full-length novel anonymously. But her feminine authorial identity was quickly perceived by at least one eminent reader. Thomas Carlyle wrote to her in 1848, 'Dear Madam, (For I catch the treble of that fine melodious voice very well). . . .'[35] But the reader addressed and whom she was most anxious to reach, was male: the manufacturing employer, the 'master'. She was deeply concerned about their response to the book.

The feminine persona of the author is established in many of the direct authorial interventions which litter the narrative. She has a recurrent refrain, her disclaimer of any knowledge of political economy. As author, she claims the right to speak not from knowledge of 'the facts' but from an identification with the feelings of an oppressed and suffering workforce. In so doing, she claims a woman's privilege. In fact Gaskell was an intelligent woman whose wide reading included works of political economy which she claimed in her authorial role not to comprehend. But it would be presumptious in a woman to speak authoritatively in a woman's voice of such matters. Where she could legitimately speak was of course from sympathetic feeling, and this is what she chose to do, at the cost of playing down her intellect.

However while the address is from a feminine position, the subject matter of the novel places it firmly in the public domain. Yet the novel is remarkably lacking in any scenes which are set in the public world of paid work and politics in spite of its concern with the relationship between masters and men. The book is almost entirely enacted in terms of the effects of this relationship upon personal and family lives. John Barton's visit to London with the chartists is told off-stage, and there is but a single scene of direct confrontation between masters and men which provides the motivation for the killing of Henry Carson. So although the original title as Williams points out, was to have been 'John Barton', '. . . the person with whom all my sympathies went . . .'[36] yet the change which foregrounds the daughter at the expense of the father is, in some respects, appropriate. For it is women and their suffering in the family which provide the angle of vision in a melodramatic plot in which that suffering can take tangible and heightened forms such as the brain fever suffered by Mary upon Jem's acquittal. It is this angle of vision on the condition of England question which legitimates Gaskell's authority to speak, to write in her authorial persona as educated, womanly sympathizer, first hand observer although an outsider, of the suffering of the working class.

Gaskell's refrain that she knows nothing of political economy is taken up by one of her key characters, Job Legh. The distance between author and character is carefully maintained, in spite of the identity of view; a distance defined in terms of class, education, and sex. The feminine author's disclaimer is by virtue of her sex, while Job Legh's is a result of his lack of education. But when Job Legh speaks out, in the penultimate chapter, it has the effect of confirming the author's contention that she speaks of the real feeling of inarticulate working men. Legh's speech is addressed to the chief representative in the novel of Gaskell's preferred reader, the 'master', Mr Carson. It is this chain of address, as well as the industrial theme, which locates the novel in the public domain in which 'literature' may be generated, inspite of its overriding concern with personal relationships and families.

Writing of Gaskell's later fiction, George Sand commented: 'Mrs Gaskell has done what neither I nor other female authors in France can accomplish — she has written novels which excite the deepest interest in men of the world and yet which every girl will be the better for reading'.[37]

The Domestic Novels; Cousin Phillis

In *Cousin Phillis* and *Wives and Daughters*, as in the earlier *Cranford*, the interest of 'men of the world' is not engaged, as it was in the Manchester novels, through a setting in the public domain and an engagement with contemporary social issues. If Sand was right, and she surely was, then Gaskell's achievement was even more impressive. It was to engage that interest in a fictional world which centred on the private, domestic and personal, the 'woman's world' which was so often the setting of woman-to-woman writing. The private worlds she created in these fictions were flattering to the men they contained, creating through them a place in which the male reader might position himself with a degree of comfort.

The goodness of Jane Austen's good heroes is dramatized through their behaviour in the private domain, as fathers, lovers and husbands. Although their goodness is defined by their actions in the world — notably their relationship to their estates — we have little sense of what the Knightleys and Darceys actually do. They are kept busy about their affairs, but off-stage. Elizabeth Gaskell's good men may perhaps be epitomized by the Rev Ebenezer Holman, Phillis's father. He is most vividly constructed in his work, both as a Dissenting minister and as a farmer, and in his keen intellectual interests. It is his stature as a man among men, outside of family life, which gives weight to his actions as a husband and father. It is he and not his daughter who is sensitive to his wife's exclusion from the interests of father and daughter: 'I was rather sorry for cousin Holman ... for do what she would, she was completely unable even to understand the pleasure her husband and daughter took in intellectual pursuits, much less to care in the least for the pursuits themselves ... I had once or twice thought she was a little jealous of her own child, as a fitter companion for her husband than she was herself; and I fancied the minister himself was aware of this feeling, for I had noticed an occasional sudden change of subject, and a tenderness of appeal in his voice as he spoke to her. ... I do not think that Phillis ever perceived these little shadows. ...'[38] It is he and not his wife who penetrates the secret of Phillis's hopeless love for Holdsworth. Gaskell creates in such characters men whose standing in the public domain amongst men is unquestioned. By making such a man sensitive as a woman was supposed to be to the nuances of family life and personal relationships, she revalues the private domain far more effectively than can ever be achieved through woman-to-woman conventions. Her method also ensured that this revaluation was achieved without provoking either the hostility which attended direct confrontation with and the refusal of, femininity, or the contempt with which the literary establishment and the world of male readers treated woman-to-woman affirmations of the value of domestic and personal life.

Domestic Ideology: Enabling or Limiting?

That this strategy was an enabling one may be amply demonstrated in Elizabeth Gaskell's case. She was able to achieve both a lasting literary reputation, tempered it is true by an unmistakable tone of condescension not unconnected with her feminine persona, and a very considerable measure of economic power. No matter that William pocketed her first cheque, and that in law her earnings belonged to him; Elizabeth Gaskell gained through her earning power the ability to determine a lifestyle which would have been quite outside his means to provide as a Unitarian minister in the provinces, and to which William Gaskell in any case does not seem to have aspired. He was happy to remain at home while his wife and daughters travelled and socialized. Yet these gains were achieved without detriment to a very full domestic life in which she took manifest pleasure.

It is ironic that Branca refused the evidence of those exceptional women who broke silence to leave records in their fiction, their diaries and their letters, of their lives, and thoughts and feelings about them. For Gaskell provides strong supporting evidence for Branca's contention that married middle-class women were both very busy and fully committed to their domestic roles. Yet the power of the stereotype of the idle lady was so strong that Gaskell herself drew upon it in her portrait of the Carson household in *Mary Barton*: 'Mrs Carson was (as usual with her, when no particular excitement was going on), very poorly, and sitting upstairs in her dressing-room ... it was but the natural consequence of the state of mental and bodily idleness in which she was placed ... it would have done her more good than all the aether and sal-volatile she was daily in the habit of swallowing if she might have taken the work of one of her own housemaids for a week. ...' Downstairs meantime her daughter '... did not exactly know what to do to while away the time until the tea-hour'.[39] The contrast between this fictional construction and its author's representation in letters of her daily life could not have been more stark: 'I have Florence and Willie in my room which is also nursery, call Hearn at six, ½p.6 she is dressed, comes in, dresses Flora, gives her breakfast the first; ½p.7 I get up, 8 Flora goes down to her sisters and Daddy, and Hearn to her breakfast. While I in my dressing gown dress Willie. ½p.8 I go to breakfast with parlour people, Florence being with us and Willie (ought to be) in his cot; Hearn makes beds etc. in nursery only. 9 she takes F. and I read chapter and have prayers first with household and then with children. ½p.9 Florence and Willie come in drawing room for an hour while bedroom and nursery windows are open; ½p.10 go in kitchen, cellars and order dinner. Write letters; ¼p.11 put on things; ½.11 take Florence out. I come in, nurse W. and get ready for dinner; ½p.2 children, two little ones, come down during servants' dinner half hour open windows upstairs; 3 p.m. go up again and I have two hours to kick my heels in. ...'[40] And so the day continues.

In the light of this kind of evidence it is simply not plausible to present domesticity as always and uniformly an oppressive imposition upon women. As feminists we need to be able to register the extent to which domestic life has had and continues to have a compelling attraction for many women. Mary Poovey is certainly correct to speak of the ideology of domesticity as enabling, a channel through which desires were satisfied. She is equally correct in identifying it as disabling and limiting. For the channel through which female desire might be legitimately expressed was narrow, and not infrequently blocked. The most striking instance in Gaskell's fiction is Phillis. Her author constructs her character endowed with brains as well as beauty. We see her learning Latin and Italian, and '... leaning over and listening greedily, with her hand on his shoulder, sucking in information like her father's own daughter',[41] — information in this case about something as unfeminine as dynamics. Her author does not comment directly on Phillis's unusual accomplishments, but allows her narrator, the young and intimidated cousin Paul, and his father, to do so:

> 'You see she's so clever — she's more like a man than a woman — she knows Latin and Greek.'
> 'She'd forget 'em, if she'd a houseful of children,' was my father's comment on this.
> 'But she knows many a thing besides, and is wise as well as learned; she has been so much with her father. She would never think much of me, and I should like my wife to think a deal of her husband. . . .'[42]

While Gaskell is careful not to endorse these sentiments of Paul's about the disadvantages of too much intelligence in a wife, neither does she ever contemplate any outlet for Phillis's energies outside of the domestic channel which is to be blocked by Holdsworth's departure for Canada. It is not the narrowness of choice open to her which we are persuaded to see and regret, but only Holdsworth's moral failure, and Phillis's grief. She falls ill of 'brain fever', and rallies, not at the prospect of some occupation for her intelligent faculties, but on the exhortation of the servant Betty that she should remember her duty to her parents. Female energy and intelligence is never given any non-domestic outlet in Gaskell's work and is often harmful in its effects, as with Miss Jenkyns in *Cranford* compared with the gentle but weakminded sister whom everyone loves, Miss Matty.

'Determinate Fears in Realist Form'

Moretti argued that the function of the literature of terror was '. . . to take up within itself determinate fears in order to present them in a form different from their real one. . . .'[43] Indeed he sees this as the function of literature in general. But if real fears can be transformed into fearful but fantastic monsters in the literature of terror, they must wear a different disguise in realist mode.

No general account of the manner in which realist fiction handles fears which cannot be fully acknowledged, whether for psychic or social reasons, is offered. But the case of *Mary Barton* is particularly interesting in the light of the monster as metaphor for the industrial proletariat proposed by Moretti. *Mary Barton* appeared some thirty years after the first edition of *Frankenstein*.

Whether or not Moretti's interpretation is one which the text itself legitimizes, it is clearly one which it suggests, for it was made by Gaskell in the pages of *Mary Barton*. Making the typical confusion of the monster with its maker, she wrote, 'The actions of the uneducated seem to me typified in those of Frankenstein, that monster of many human qualities, ungifted with a soul. ... The people rise up to life; they irritate us, they terrify us, and we become their enemies. Then, in the sorrowful moment of our triumphant power, their eyes gaze on us with mute reproach. Why have we made them as they are; a powerful monster, yet without the inner means for peace and happiness? John Barton became a Chartist, a Communist ...'[44] — a monster, and like Frankenstein's monster, a murderer.

If we accept for the moment the idea that the social class which capitalism itself both produces and fears, the working class, may figure in bourgeois literature of terror as a hideous and fearful monster, then if it is to appear and express that fear in realist fiction, it must be in a form which is recognizable, not disguised as a non-human monster. A condition of the appearance of real fears in recognizable form in realist fiction would seem to be that the fear must be formulated in such a way that it may be overcome in the course of the narrative. In *Frankenstein* the monster which figures the fear is beyond any hope of integration into society even on its own modest reformist terms, because it is alien, non-human. The fear can be expressed in radical form, as unresolvable, *because* it is disguised. Where it appears undisguised, then the real threat which it acknowledges must be shown to be one which can be contained. In *Mary Barton* the monster is human. Unlike Shelley's hideous progeny, it is part of and must be included within, the human 'brotherhood'. It can take form as a creature who can be viewed sympathetically because it can be shown to be, potentially, at least, 'just like us' (the bourgeoisie) and because political economy teaches us that in the long run its interests, too, are bound up with the fortunes of capitalism. In realist form, the monster is one which may be educated, tamed, accepted and loved, in spite of its fearful mien.

Which is the more or less 'subversive' or conformist? The fantasy form because the fear may be represented more radically, with no possibility of reconciliation? Or the realist form because the fear is recognizable and named for what it is? It could be argued either way. In spite of the moment when the monster speaks out to such effect upon the glacier, the reader cannot in the last resort side with the monster, because he *is* monstrous. But there is less secure protection against a transfer of sympathy to the monster humanized and made recognizable. *Mary Barton* provoked considerable controversy and resentment among the 'masters', who complained bitterly of its one-sided sympathies. It is doubtful whether the same men would have felt threatened in any way had Gaskell produced instead a mythical monster in a fantastic tale. Yet by the same token, the realist form permitted the fear to be formulated in terms which placed it within the frame of the dominant ideology, and therefore in terms in which it could be resolved and, at least partially, dissolved.

5.

Nineteenth-Century Feminism and Fiction, I

It was argued in the last chapter that the ideology of domesticity in the nineteenth century could not be seen as an alien and oppressive imposition upon middle-class women — a narrow straitjacket which men forced them to wear. Neither could it be seen as a set of garments willingly donned by the silent sisterhood and worn with no consciousness of tight corsets and constricted feet. Rather the ideology set the terms within or against which women had to negotiate their sexed identity and their social relationships. And it was backed by punitive legal and social sanctions which made open defiance a costly and painful business.

The terms of the ideology of domesticity necessarily affected the ways in which the campaigns of the nineteenth-century women's movement were fought. Instead of setting up a clear division between a silent majority who conformed willingly: those, in Mary Poovey's phrase, whose desires seemed more or less commensurate with their duties, and a noisy minority of 'exceptional women' who stepped outside the confines to engage in feminist protest, it is interesting to consider ways in which even women who were most fully caught up in domestic femininity might respond to and even initiate movements of reform which could become quite radical.

The nineteenth-century women's movement generated by and large a moderate feminism which developed along the lines of fault of the dominant domestic ideology. It explored the internal

95

contradictions of that ideology and opened up new opportunities for middle-class women in the public domain of work and politics. The major fault-lines had to do with the plight of the single woman; with that of ill-treated or deserted wives; with the sexual double-standard and the doctrine of female moral superiority; and with philanthropy.

Single Women

Branca challenged the widely held view among feminists and others that there was a crisis over single women in the latter half of the nineteenth century.[1] She cited marriage statistics to show that the vast majority of bourgeois women married at some point in their lives, and that the marriage rate had not changed significantly in the period of supposed crisis when compared to earlier rates. However she failed to confront some important questions. There is undeniable evidence of a perceived crisis at this time of such severe magnitude that draconic solutions, such as the exporting of so-called surplus women to the colonies where they were in short supply, were not only proposed but acted upon.[2] The plight of the single woman was a commonplace topic of debate and public concern. If there was no real change behind this perceived crisis, there was nevertheless a moral panic about her which stands in need of some explanation. The significance of the single woman should be sought not in social statistics but in the space where she had suddenly become defined as a problem — the space of ideology.

Domestic ideology and the system of gender relations it legitimated had literally no place for the single woman. She was unprovided for in theory and practice. The plight of the single woman had long since been registered in the fiction of women who found themselves in this situation. Jane Austen's greatest novel, *Emma*, hinges on the episode in which the rich and spoilt heroine is rude to the middle-aged and garrulous Miss Bates on the outing to Boxhill. The vulnerability of the gentry ideology to which Jane Austen subscribed with respect to the single woman was tacitly recognized by making Emma's attitude to a powerless single woman of her class the final acid test of the worth of the heroine. Charlotte Brontë was very conscious of the single woman struggling to maintain caste and to find a meaningful occupation in a life in which domestic fulfilment was blocked. However Brontë would certainly have been counted by Branca among those exceptional women who, unlike the silent majority, were not content to be daughters, wives and mothers. In a much-quoted letter to Southey she wrote: '... I have endeavoured not only attentively to observe all the duties a woman ought to fulfil, but to feel deeply interested in them. I don't always succeed, for sometimes when I'm teaching or sewing I would rather be reading or writing'.[3] Yet if we turn to Elizabeth Gaskell, who was constantly singing the praises of marriage, motherhood and domesticity, we find in both her work and her life an uneasy consciousness of the plight of the single woman. *Cousin Phillis* is one of her most moving stories, and one of the simplest. Her heroine is exceptionally gifted, and the novel's plot might have hinged around the problem of finding scope for exercising her intelligence within the confines of domesticity. Instead as we have seen, the story's tragedy lies in Phillis's desertion by the man she has come to love. It is the lost opportunity to exercise maternal and wifely affections which is mourned and not the lack of any other outlet for her energy and talent. The ironically labelled 'amazonian' world of *Cranford* is suffused through and through with a sense of loss and waste occasioned by the gentle Miss Matty's spinsterhood. Unlike Phillis, Miss Matty had the aptitude for nothing but domestic life, certainly not for her short career in importing and selling tea. But her author leaves us in no doubt that a marriage to the lover her family coerced her into rejecting in her youth, would have given infinitely more scope for the exercise of domestic affections than her subsequent existence with father and sister in the rural setting of Cranford, however lovingly and positively it was portrayed.

Elizabeth Gaskell had four daughters, only two of whom married. Thanks to her own earning power as a writer, her unmarried daughters were provided for without the need to enter paid employment, as they surely would have had to had the household depended entirely on William's earnings.[4] Even such a partisan of marriage and domesticity could not fail to be conscious therefore of the need to give young women the means to provide for themselves outside of marriage. Such a woman could not fail to respond to the plea for improved educational opportunities for her sex, and for the opening up of 'respectable' fields of employment for the Miss Jenkyns, the Phillises and the Miss Gaskells of her world.

The single woman became the focus of intense ideological struggle at the point in time when her plight began to be seen as unnecessary. Feminist campaigns to open up new fields of employment and training to women gained enormously from the existence of the class of single women. The success of the movement for women's education depended not on parents who wished to give their daughters the choice whether or not to marry, but on those who wished no better future for them, but who saw the wisdom of providing a fail-safe, and who were willing to be persuaded that there was no necessary conflict between education and domesticity.

The campaign to educate young women, and to offer them career opportunities should they 'fail' to marry, was one which could and did secure the support of many women and men who would not have questioned the desirability of marriage for their daughters. But if women who situated themselves relatively comfortably within the feminine persona and role offered by domestic ideology might nevertheless appreciate the need to provide the means for single women to support themselves, other women who found those roles less comfortable had additional incentives for welcoming the campaign for work, education and independence for single women. Such women might and did see in education and a career, not a fail-safe but an alternative, one which might give them the option of choosing not to marry even where they might do so if they wished.

It was surely the fear that the first motivation might be a cover for the second; that women might use the fail-safe as an escape route which would allow them to evade their 'natural' feminine duties, that provoked the widespread resistance to women's education. Male defenders of domestic ideology sometimes went to absurd lengths: 'We ought always to clearly bear in mind — men and women alike — that to all time the vast majority of women must be wives and mothers; that on those women who became wives and mothers depends the future of the race; and that if either class must be sacrificed to the other, it is the spinsters whose type perishes with them who should be sacrificed to the matrons who carry on the life and qualities of the species. . . .'[5]

'It is not in the interest of States ... to encourage the existence, as a rule, of women who are other than entirely dependent on man as well for subsistence as for protection and love.

Married life is a woman's profession; and to this life her training — that of dependence — is modelled. Of course by not getting a husband, or losing him, she may find that she is without resources. All that can be said of her is, she has failed in business ... The mischance of the distressed governess and the unprovided widow, is that of every insolvent tradesman. He is to be pitied ... but it would be just as reasonable to demand that every boy be taught two or three professions because he may fail in one, as it is to argue that all our social habits should be changed because one woman in fifty — or whatever the statistics are — is a spinster or widow without any resources.'[6]

The bottom line of the ideology of domesticity, as with most ideological constructions of femininity, is the appeal to nature. Yet the fear which is exposed in the resistance to women's education and training above reveals a different state of affairs. For in fact neither type of woman need have been sacrificed to the other. Women might be prepared for domestic life, yet be trained for other eventualities. What was revealed by the refusal to countenance the education of women so that they might support themselves if they did not marry was the fear that, given a choice, women might flout 'nature'. If femininity and domestic life comes naturally to women by virtue of their sex, then there would be no need to train them to accept it, nor to offer any compulsions to conformity. What is revealed is the fear that, after all, feminine conformity is the work of nurture combined with compulsion and material interest, and that nature has very little to do with it.

The explosion of 'the marriage debate' some time after women had gained the right of entry to higher education, and when new areas of paid employment were beginning to open up, suggests that these fears may have rested on an uneasy sense of the frustrations and dissatisfaction of many married women, which must have been evident in private long before it was expressed in public. In August 1888, Mona Caird wrote an article in the *Daily Telegraph* which triggered a flood of correspondence on marriage.[7] And the woman's 'new woman' fiction of the eighteen-nineties foregrounded the figure of the heroine who was 'a victim of matrimony'. Marriage and the oppression of women within it was placed high on the agenda of the women's movement.

The process by which the logic of domestic ideology becomes unpicked when quite modest demands are made which do not on the face of it offer any challenge to its terms, reveals the radicalizing potential of the nineteenth-century campaigns for reform. Campaigners who began their activities in seemly modesty and with feminine decorum, were deeply shocked by the misogynist rage and hatred which their demands could provoke. More radical feminisms were the predictable outcome of this experience.

Deserted or Ill-Treated Wives

Nineteenth-century domestic ideology legitimated marriage relationships which placed women, formally at least, in positions of near total dependency on their husbands and fathers. The law denied the married woman any right to her own property, and even to the proceeds of her own labour. She lacked political representation, and not being a legal person, could not initiate legal actions on her own behalf. She had no custodial rights over her children before 1839, when limited reforms were introduced.[8] This total dependency was justified in terms of her need for male protection. If women were constitutionally and naturally unfit to care for themselves, then it was in their own best interests that they should be denied the means to make the attempt. Male power over wives and daughters would be exercised benevolently in their own best interests and out of love for them. Romantic love complemented domestic ideology, shoring up its weak places. The hope of inspiring such love must have contributed to the maintenance of the erotic charge of male power.

However the second line of fault in domestic ideology concerned those wives who had had abused this power over them vested in their husbands. Campaigns for legal reform respecting child custody, access, divorce, and married women's property rights all foregrounded the plight of the deserted or ill-treated wife. While this certainly strengthened the case, it had the unfortunate effect that the tacit assumption was often left standing that, these being exceptional cases, the situation of wives who were not ill-treated or deserted created no cause for concern.

Many of the campaigners hoped that reforms whose necessity could be most forcibly demonstrated in these cases would meliorate the situation of all wives. In fact the basic situation of the married woman who remained married changed only very slowly, in part because of this reform focus on special cases. The sexual double-standard inscribed in the provisions of the Marriage and Divorce Bill of 1857 under which a man might divorce his wife on grounds of adultery alone, while she had to cite additional causes such as desertion or cruelty, was not eradicated until 1923. The first Married Women's Property Bill, introduced in 1857, failed and women did not gain full rights over property until 1881. The first Infant Custody Act of 1839 gave deserted wives strictly limited rights over children under seven and of access to older children — provided they were 'virtuous'. They did not gain equitable treatment in this matter until 1925.

The Double-Standard, and Female Moral Superiority

This doctrine of the innate virtue of the female which was used to rationalize the sexual double-standard, was one which was used to police them. For if virtue came 'naturally' to women, then offences against virtue were all the more heinous in a woman. Virtue was enjoined on men, too, but as it came harder to them, then lapses might be excused, even expected. Hence the thinking incorporated in the Divorce Bill. However the doctrine could also be turned to women's advantage. Women reformers turned the male logic on its head, to argue that vice in all its worst forms was principally caused by men, who were on their own admission more naturally prone to it than women. Purity campaigns in which non-conformist women were prominent, centred on the evils of drink and prostitution. But where the penal system blamed the prostitute, feminist campaigners such as Josephine Butler turned the spotlight on her clients. If women had little or no sexual urge, and were naturally inclined to virtue, then the reason for their turning to vice must be sought in the destitution which drove them to it, in their seduction and betrayal by men, and in male sexual incontinence which was the source of the demand. The campaign for the repeal of the Contagious Diseases Acts exemplified a common attribute of many feminist campaigns of the time, the insistence that indeed women were morally superior to men, and that men must raise themselves to the standards set by women. In the absence of male reform, then women stood in need of protection against men rather than from them.[9]

The Contagious Diseases campaign is another good example of the radicalizing effect of reform movements whose initial starting point lay well within the confines of domestic ideology. The movement provoked great hostility. But in addition to the radicalizing effect of the shock produced by hostile outbursts, the campaign against the Acts had political educational value, in that it brought middle-class women into direct contact with the Acts' working-class victims. The sexual double-standard might also be revealed as a class double-standard. No one with first hand knowledge of the way in which working-class prostitutes were abused, both in the courts and in the Lock hospitals, as well as by middle-class seducers and clients, could fail to mark the gulf between this abuse and the veneration with which the middle-class angel-in-the-house was regarded, at least in theory. It was but a small further step to make the connection between the physical and sexual abuse of working-class women, and the rage and hatred provoked by the most controversial middle-class feminist campaigns.

Of all of these, none provoked this response to a greater degree than the campaign against the Contagious Diseases Acts. Josephine Butler records the reaction to an attempt to speak to this topic in the course of the Pontefract by-election in 1872: 'Mrs Wilson and I stood in front of the company of women, side by side. She whispered in my ear, "Now is the time to trust in God; do not let us fear"; and a comforting sense of the Divine presence came to us both. It was not personal violence that we feared so much as the mental pain inflicted by the rage, profanity and obscenity of the men, of their words and their threats. Their language was hideous. They shook their fists in our faces, with volleys of oaths. This continued for some time, and we had no defence or means of escape. ... The new teaching and revolt of women had stirred up the very depths of hell. We said nothing, for our voices could not have been heard. We simply stood shoulder to shoulder. ...'[10]

Philanthropy

The one field in which women could legitimately enter into public affairs was that of philanthropy, and many involved themselves in a variety of charitable enterprises, such as prison-visiting, public health and housing reform movements, voluntary missions dispensing charity and 'friendship' to the poor, the education of poor children in voluntary schools, and so on. At one level these women may be seen as constituting an ideological army, agents for the dissemination of ideas and practices among the working class calculated to secure bourgeois hegemony. The temperence movement for instance is often presented in this light, as an attack on working-class political institutions, since the public house was perhaps *the* major institution of the 'proletarian public sphere', where political and trades union mobilization occurred. The philanthropic drive to improve the home life of the 'deserving poor' by teaching working-class wives standards of modest comfort also had an eye to the desirable side-effect of providing a buffer against working-class radicalism. If men had comfortable homes to go to, then they might be less attracted to drink and to political agitation.

But just as Taylor demonstrates that domestic ideology had positive attractions for working-class wives, and therefore cannot be seen simply as an alien imposition foisted on them in the interest of bourgeois hegemony, so too the effects of philanthropy on bourgeois women were not unidirectional.[11] For the same movement which aimed to teach working-class wives to become traditional homemakers — plain clothes angels-in-the house — took bourgeois women out of their own homes and gave them a valuable political education. It gave them first hand knowledge of the conditions of working-class life, and it brought them into conflict with those men of their own class who opposed the access of women to positions of authority on public boards and governing bodies. Middle-class women were drawn into public life as a result of these activities, particularly at the level of local government administration, and this experience was vital as a step towards gaining the franchise.

The Double-Bind of Nineteenth-Century Feminism

Many of the campaigns of the nineteenth-century women's movement, then, began from modest reformist demands framed within the terms of domestic ideology. They gained support among women who were not necessarily inclined to dispute the naturalness or the desirability of domesticity for women — at least initially. But because they opened up the lines of fault of that ideology and because they provoked such hostility, these campaigns frequently educated their participants into a more radical politics.

But because so many of the campaigns were framed within the logic of domestic ideology itself, they had the disadvantage of implicitly or explicitly reaffirming some of its central tenets. And at more than one point, the interests of one category of women were sacrificed to those of another. In 1857, the two campaigns for legal reform should have been complementary and mutually reinforcing. But the Divorce Bill was amended, largely as a result of the campaign conducted by Caroline Norton, to give divorced and separated wives some minimal rights over property and earnings. The gains which accrued to 'injured wives' were pitifully small. They included protection against her husband's claims to her earnings; the right to inherit property accrued after the separation, without resumption of property acquired before or during the marriage; the right to sue or be sued; and the possibility of gaining maintenance.[12] But they were gained at the expense of wives who were not 'wronged'. For the concessions were used to kill the Married Women's Property Bill. Reticence in challenging the power of husbands in marriage for fear of being seen to challenge the institution itself was disastrous in this case.

A second instance in which the movement was divided was over suffrage. Feminists were in disagreement over the question of votes for married women, again for fear of sowing dissension between man and wife. Millicent Fawcett was one prominent feminist who took this view of the matter. She wrote in 1889 that 'The case for the enfranchisement of women who are standing alone and bearing the burden of citizenship as ratepayers and taxpayers, seems unanswerable. ... The enfranchisement of wives is an altogether different question'.[13]

Finally, the overriding necessity of demonstrating that the

demands of the campaigners might be met without destroying 'womanliness' or feminine respectability, led to a number of failures of mutual support between different campaigns. The chief sufferers here were the campaigns for the repeal of the Contagious Diseases Acts, and for birth control. But even less highly sensitive areas such as the campaign for higher education for women suffered very real disabilities because of the desire to allay the fear that the education of women would make them 'mannish'.

Olive Banks sums up the position that so much of the nineteenth-century woman's movement found itself boxed into: '... feminism was trapped into a view of womanhood that came dangerously close to the traditional view from which the feminists were trying to escape'.[14] But there is a more fundamental cause behind the self-imposed constraints under which most of the campaigns were conducted. It lies in the relationship between feminism and class. Feminism could not become revolutionary with respect to the prevailing gender-order without also challenging the class order, because of the way that class-identity had become bound up with gender-differentiation. The majority of feminists were by no means social revolutionaries. Few were fighting for the emancipation of the working class as well as of women. It was for this reason that many women revolutionaries, such as Alexandra Kollontai in Russia, dissociated themselves from feminism.[15] What most wanted was the improvement of their own position without loss of caste. However they were hamstrung in this endeavour by the complex manner in which bourgeois status was articulated, defined, and marked off from both gentry 'decadence' and working-class 'vulgarity' by the norms of gender derived from domestic ideology.[16] In order not to lose caste it was essential that they maintained their standing as 'ladies', and to do this they must backhandedly affirm prevailing gender identities. They must show that 'true womanliness' would remain unaffected by education or the vote, or paid employment of a 'respectable' kind. And above all, they had to tread most carefully with respect to the sacred heartland of domestic ideology, the family and motherhood.

Feminism and Fiction: the Literary Harvest

The literary beneficiaries of nineteenth-century feminism were men rather than women. At the time there were a number of feminist writers who were active in the women's movement and whose work was immensely popular; for example, Mona Caird, Sarah Grand, Olive Schreiner, and George Egerton. Schreiner was 'rediscovered' a number of times in the course of the twentieth century and she has an honourable, if minor, place in the literary histories. But most of the others are now known if at all only through recent feminist reprint series such as the Virago Modern Classics. The male writers of 'new woman' fiction gained entry into the literary history books and stayed there, regardless of the fluctuating fortunes of the women's movement.

Patricia Stubbs's study of feminism and fiction in the period 1880-1920 graphically illustrates this perhaps surprising instance of male literary dominance. It is a book which, despite its title, is almost entirely devoted to the work of men whether she is considering the positive response to feminism in fiction or the rearguard counterattack.[17] Gail Cunningham devotes the first half of her study of new woman fiction primarily to women, but attributes to them only a necessary function in sweeping away '. . . the constricting bounds of conventional reticence' to help '. . . clear a path for better novelists to tread relatively unmolested'.[18] These 'better novelists' are all however male. John Goode's essay on feminism and the literary text in this period might almost give the impression of an inverse ratio between the sex of the writers and literary feminism.[19] The authors rated most highly are the familiar trio discussed by Cunningham and Stubbs: Hardy, Meredith and Gissing. It is these men who have come to represent new woman fiction in the literary histories.

Goode argues that these three men came closest to achieving a level of literary coherence which had as its condition the exposure of ideological incoherences, while those who reversed this order to produce ideological coherence at the expense of the literary variety include the only two women writers he discusses, Eliza Lynn Linton and Mrs Oliphant. The only women he mentions therefore belong to the camp of the opponents of feminism. He does not mention any of the women writers who were feminists.

These points are not made in a critical spirit, or necessarily in disagreement with the literary judgements being made. I, too, have found how difficult it is to avoid making just the same choices. The question posed is why it was that the men who took up the themes of feminism in their fiction were the ones who had literary survival value, and not the women. Was it, pace Spender, simply another instance of the male rip-off, covered by a male literary critical establishment? Possibly; but then we are forced to confront another question. Why was it that Austen, the Brontës, Eliot and Gaskell were able to produce novels which escaped this process of appropriation and suppression?

It was suggested in the last chapter that a condition imposed on candidates for literary canonization was that they avoided woman-to-woman discourse. The first possibility that therefore suggests itself is that women writers of feminist fiction addressed only women, and therefore were automatically discounted. However the contemporary interest in 'the woman question' ensured a very wide readership for these novels. While they certainly were addressed to women who were perhaps their preferred readers, they were also addressed, many of them, to men, and were read by men.

Before returning to this question in a moment, let us look at one or two examples of men's new woman fiction.

Odd Women and Ill-Assorted Couples

'I hope to finish with the delivery of the terrible woman afflicting me (a positive heroine with brains, with real blood ...) by the end of April.

'I could have killed her merrily, with my compliments to the public; and that was my intention. But the marrying of her, sets me traversing genuine labyrinths ... the coupling of such a woman and her man is a delicate business'.[20] So wrote George Meredith in 1884 of the heroine of his *Diana of the Crossways*. She was based in part on Caroline Norton, *cause célèbre* of the campaigns for child custody and the rights of deserted and separated wives, and certain notorious incidents in her life provided Meredith with material for his plot. But she also resembled Meredith's first wife who had left him in 1858 for another man, and whom he had denied access to their son until shortly before her death in 1861.[21]

Meredith's Diana is a figure who inspires a certain amount of anxiety in the male protagonists of the novel and also, it would seem from the Lindsay quotation, in her author. In the opening chapter she is constructed for us entirely at second hand, through extracts from diarists who offer accounts of her beauty and instances of her wit. Subsequently introduced to us in person at a social gathering in Dublin in the second chapter, her beauty and the small fracas she unwittingly causes among would-be rivals, identify her as 'in the market', as her friend Emmy puts it, but simultaneously her wit marks her as a threat and a challenge to any man tempted to purchase. Any display of cleverness in a woman is liable to provoke unease, as it does not sit well with the image of the angel-in-the-house. Even when the would-be patriarch is not the immediate object, feminine wit may strike him with anxiety, for it evidences an intelligent subjectivity which belies both passivity and inferiority. If irony is, as Judy Simons claims, 'the woman's weapon against the male regime',[22] then it serves as well in social interaction as in fiction to distance women from the claims of that regime.

All the men in Diana's life are uncomfortable in the face of her wit when they place themselves in imagination or in actuality as her consort. The unseen husband, Warwick, modelled on Caroline Norton's husband, George ('... stifler, lung contractor, iron mask, inquisitor ...'), is regarded with a sneaking sympathy by Diana's suitor, Dacier: 'She might be a devil of a wife'.[23] '... delightful to hear, delightful to see', yet 'so clever a woman might be too clever for her friends!'[24] Clearly Warwick had found her so. Diana comments that he had '... suffered under my "sallies": and it was the worse for him when he did not perceive their drift. ... I "rendered" him ridiculous — I had caught a trick of "using men's phrases"'.[25] (A charge not without foundations incidently: later in the novel we find her entertaining another suitor, Redworth, in order to extract current political gossip and comment which she passes on to Dacier as her own.) Redworth, too, although more willing to 'play second to her', reflects that 'A quick-witted woman exerting her wit is both a foreigner and potentially a criminal' and that her wit might have accounted 'for her husband's discontent — the reduction of him to a state of mere masculine antagonism. What is the husband of a vanward woman? He feels himself but a diminished man'.[26] Redworth, like Warwick, cannot always perceive her drift, and Diana's friend Emma Dunstance catches him out in incomprehension at the Dublin ball: 'Lady Dunstance . . . glanced up at Mr Redworth, whose brows bore the knot of perplexity over a strong stare. He, too, stamped the words on his memory to see subsequently whether they had a vestige of meaning'.[27]

Redworth, unlike Dacier and Warwick, can take the risk of 'playing second' to Diana however because he has had a privileged glimpse of a very different persona — the altogether more malleable figure of the Victorian angel-in-the-house. In an early crisis, he follows her on horseback to Crossways of the title, where he is rewarded by a vision of Diana as angel as he watches her light a fire: 'Redworth eyed Diana in the first fire-glow. He could have imagined a Madonna on an old black Spanish canvas. The act of servitude was beautiful in graceful-ness, and her simplicity in doing the work touched it spiritually . . . it required the superbness of her beauty and the contrasting charm of her humble posture of kneeling by the fire, to set him on his right track of mind. He knew and was sure of her'.[28] The vision, like the advertisement, reassures that despite alarming appearances of independence and intelligence, 'underneath they're all loveable'. The vision glimpsed by Redworth is given further support when Diana nurses Emma through brutal surgery. Finally her independence is shown to be illusory. Redworth attempts behind the scenes to ensure that her novels will be successful by using his influence to promote them.

It is the vision of Diana as angel which underwrites Meredith's plot resolution of a second marriage to the dull but worthy Redworth, one which many have thought a betrayal of his heroine to which the death the author entertained would have been a more satisfactory alternative. While John Goode rightly claims that Meredith would merely have swopped one myth for another had he allowed Diana to escape the 'cont-iguities of her situation' into an absolute freedom as an inde-pendent woman,[29] nevertheless he might have spared us and her the spectacle of her 'freely subjecting herself' to such a non-entity. And the ambiguous structure of feeling which Meredith creates around Diana as independent woman and as angel, must leave a doubt whether the resolution was as strictly determined by the demands of fictional integrity as Goode suggests. Jack

Lindsay's account of Meredith's second wife, successor to the first in whose likeness Diana was moulded, might also lead to some hesitation as to the degree of distance between Redworth when he falls under the spell of the vision of Diana kneeling in lovely servitude, and his author: 'She had no strong or vital character, and was not particularly intellectual or beautiful. ... No doubt after his experience of Mary Nicholls, which had hit him so hard, a woman like Marie Vulliamy, with her passive femininity ... was best calculated to fill his life harmoniously and give him the aid he needed'.[30] Not a woman, it seems, to whom there would be any necessity to play second. Meredith too, perhaps, like Diana's suitors, understood the fear that such a woman might prove 'a devil of a wife', and might have a sneaking sympathy for his male protagonist's preference for the more traditional and less threatening angel and helpmeet of domestic ideology.

The structure of feeling which Meredith creates in *Diana of the Crossways* is one not unfamiliar today among contemporary friends of feminism; political and intellectual support and sympathy for feminism, combined with fear and resentment of the new, independent woman. The fear is allayed in the course of Meredith's narrative, by the uncovering of a more familiar and less threatening figure who can still love and be loved. The unlovable face of the new woman is nowhere more in evidence than in Gissing's *Odd Women*. Unlike Diana, Rhoda Nunn is never reduced by her author to unthreatening 'womanliness'. She remains tough and indigestible to the end — for her author, as well as for her prospective consort, Everard Barfoot, at a guess. Gissing has considerable difficulty in finding a plot structure and resolution adequate to this uncompromising heroine.

The New Woman who began to stalk so stridently through the literature of this period in the wake of the women's movement is a figure who belongs as much to anti-feminist reaction as to feminism. For the anti-feminist she is not really a woman at all, but a man in the clothing and the body of a woman. She is an Awful Warning to men and women alike, of the unnatural consequences which will ensue if women are given rights and roles which are natural only for men.

Rhoda Nunn has many of the traits of the anti-feminist New Woman, and Stubbs places Gissing among the anti-feminist misogynists in her literary construction of nineteenth-century feminism. It is, if this is the case, something of an irony that *Odd Women* should have been reprinted in the Virago Modern Classics series. Yet Gissing's is certainly a critical realism, and his deep hostility to the marriage practices of his class, and towards 'femininity', gives him some common ground with feminism, inspite of his misogyny.[31] His realism is used not to construct a fictional world which aligns itself in perfect harmony with the dominant ideology, but rather one which is used to expose it. He confronts domestic ideology with its own impossibility as a way of life, and with the effects it has on those who try to live it out.

The Odd Women constitutes a devastating fictional dissection of domestic ideology and middle-class marriage. It is structured around a passionate hatred of femininity and feminine dependence, seen not so much or not only in terms of its crippling effects upon women but as an intolerable burden on men. Almost all the early exchanges in the novel between Rhoda and Everard Barfoot concern the male victims of feminine inanity or worse. He tells her anecdotes of a Mr Poppleton, whose wife's dullness drove him into a lunatic asylum; of Mr Orchard, whose wife could discourse only on her difficulties with domestic servants, and who chose flight from her as the only alternative to suicide. Rhoda's response to these stories is to blurt out 'Why will men marry fools?'[32] Finally, when Everard threatens to give his sister-in-law, whom he blames for the death of his brother, Tom, a public whipping, Rhoda views the prospect with equanimity, even excitement: 'I think many women deserve to be beaten and ought to be beaten. . . .'[33]

This is the sentiment of two characters, and is not, of course, necessarily that of their author. But the way that the 'odd women' are positioned in the fiction suggests that the author sees them primarily in terms of the problems they create for their menfolk. If women were to gain independence, the organization of the plot suggests, then the burden of the odd women would be removed from the shoulders of young men. Sisters, sisters-in-law, maiden aunts, widowed mothers, prevent young men from marrying unless they command very considerable means. If such women could support themselves, then the men who presently support them could marry. Moreover the more intelligent of them would not be constrained to 'marry fools', but could choose educated women, their intellectual equals and fit companions for their husbands. Women, too, of course, are to be beneficiaries. They will have the possibility of useful lives whether they marry or not, and if they fail to find husbands, they will not fall into narrow poverty or destitution, even prostitution, for lack of means of support. And paradoxically, their chances of marriage will increase, because once unburdened of the odd women who must be supported in idleness, then 'odd men' will be more able and willing to marry.

This is Gissing's utopian programme, inspired by the efforts of women such as those of Langham Place who offered training along the lines of Mary Barfoot's school.[34] But despite its title, the novel is centrally concerned not with single women but with marriage. Gissing dissects middle-class marriage norms through the creation of a network of interacting couples who between them explore all the options which Gissing's fictional world presents as possible within the constraints of bourgeois standards. At the very centre of the network Gissing places a couple of minor characters whose marriage is exemplary, and who are the only happily married couple of the narrative. Micklethwaite is the acceptable face of Victorian paternalism, his wife, Fanny, the perfect angel-in-the-house. To his credit, Gissing presents this couple without the slightest trace of irony in spite of the fact that we see them through the eyes of the cynical Barfoot. Micklethwaite is 'of the Ruskin school' but is a typical male victim of middle-class marriage practices informed by the Ruskinian ideology of domesticity. He met and fell in love with Fanny when both were aged twenty-three, some seventeen years before the opening of the narrative. As a poor teacher he was unable to support a wife and family. And along with Fanny he would have acquired the familiar retinue of odd women who trail most of the characters of the novel — in this case, a widowed mother and two unsupported sisters, one of whom was blind. At the age of forty and by dint of his good fortune in securing the sale of a mathematics textbook and the ill-fortune of Fanny's dependents who, with the exception of the blind sister, have since died, seventeen years of romantic love are finally requited; devotion and fidelity, those so Ruskinian virtues, rewarded. Barfoot records for us the transformation of the Micklethwaite household effected by his faded angel. We are told of 'a domestic atmosphere that told soothingly on his nerves'; of a 'little servant' of 'gentle, noiseless demeanor which was no doubt the result of careful discipline'; of a house '. . . improved in many ways . . . in simple good taste', and of a Micklethwaite who has learned '. . . to sit on a chair like ordinary mortals' and to refrain from smoking in this haven home. 'Barfoot', his friend confides, 'there are angels walking the earth in this our day.'[35] Here is Ruskin's ideal realized, it seems. Yet it is hardly what Ruskin had in mind, and provides no model for marriage in any viable society. For societies must reproduce themselves and Fanny's most fertile years lie behind her, in a seventeen-year long celibate engagement.

Widdowson, Monica's middle-aged suitor, is another less sympathetic character who is of the Ruskin school, as Monica discovers to her cost when she marries him. There are a number of parallels between Widdowson and Micklethwaite. He too was in low paid 'respectable' employment in his youth as a clerk, and would not have been in a position to marry and support a family in gentility. But unlike Micklethwaite, Widdowson had no patient, loving Fanny with whom to share the accretion of more ample means in his middle years, after an unexpected inheritance from his brother. He chooses instead the youthful Monica, and wins her because Monica can see no other escape from oddness. In accepting Widdowson, Monica settles for half the package which domestic ideology promises to women; material support but without romantic love. She finds that in the absence of this lubricant, the ties of patriarchal authority bind intolerably tight. She seeks the missing portion in her reckless affair with Bevis. But just as Widdowson can only offer support, so Bevis can only offer romance. Each part of the package needs the other in order to be viable. By splitting it in this way, domestic ideology is exposed and dissected.

Bevis is thirty when we meet him, and we and Monica are informed by his doting mother that he has been the sole support of his three sisters and herself for some seven years — at the age at which Micklethwaite, seventeen years earlier, had been unable to marry Fanny. So by implication even where, as in the case of Bevis, a young man is successful early in his career, the odd women he supports prevent him from seeking a wife: 'It struck Monica as a very hard fate that he should have this family on his hands. What they must cost him! Probably he could not think of marrying on their account'.[36]

Through his construction of this fictional network of couples,

Gissing is able to suggest that, with the exception of the very prosperous, the prevailing domestic ideology creates the situation where those men who may inspire romantic love are typically not in a position to marry because they cannot offer support, while those who can offer support typically cannot inspire romantic love. The Monicas of this world, young women without education and training which would open access to the means of supporting themselves through paid employment of a respectable kind, are presented with a narrow range of gloomy alternatives. By thus narrowing their choices, Gissing is able to present his own preferred solution — education and training for independence — in its most favourable light.

This resolution would seem to unravel the whole unhappy situation. But it depends on an evasion on Gissing's part. There is a systematic ambiguity in his concept of independence and its meaning is never interrogated. For the women who are pupils in Mary Barfoot's school, independence means the freedom to sell their labour power without loss of caste. For men such as Barfoot and Widdowson, it means freedom *from* the necessity to sell their labour-power; they are men of 'independent means'. Both men are freed by inheritance to marry and have families, while maintaining a comfortable lifestyle; the women who become 'independent' will free their brothers to marry, but must themselves remain celibate, eking out materially restricted lives in mean lodgings such as those occupied by Monica and Mildred Vespar. Both Barfoot and Widdowson would have judged such necessitous lives as slavery rather than independence, and rightly so. Monica, in choosing a marriage of convenience to Widdowson in preference to this existence, may choose unwisely but acts in her own material best interests. For there can be no doubt that she could never hope to achieve as a result of the sale of her own labour-power the level of modest comfort which was hers as Widdowson's wife.

Gissing is much clearer about the difference between independence and economic slavery in another novel where men are more to the foreground. In *New Grub Street* the reduction of literary production to low paid drudgery for the market is presented as a species of slavery. But if to write for a living is slavery for men, then Gissing cannot in all conscience present the kind of work for which Mary and Rhoda are training young women as anything more. Clearly Gissing is recognizing here the class claims of the writer, as John Goode suggests. The rightful place of the bourgois intellectual is '... his secure insertion into the middle-class for whom he writes'.[37] But it is, equally, special pleading for the rights of bourgeois *males*. *The Odd Women* implies that Monica, Mildred Vespar, and all the others who pass through Rhoda and Mary's school, do not have class claims of the same order, but should be thankful for the opportunity to earn a meagre living which the Barfoots, Widdowsons, Micklethwaites and Bevises would see as dreary servitude for themselves.

The Monica-Widdowson-Bevis tragedy, played out around the static figure of Micklethwaite's Ruskinian marriage, is however only the subplot of the novel. The main story concerns a different type of couple, more equally matched. Both are independent in the manner of their sex. That is to say, Rhoda works for her living, while Barfoot lives off the inheritance acquired on the death of his brother Tom. And almost alone of all the characters in the novel, neither trails any dependent odd women to restrict their freedom of choice. They are therefore freed to explore Gissing's utopia, a union of equals outside the constraints of financial exigency and ideological orthodoxy.

Rhoda Nunn is the only principled odd woman in Gissing's entire collection: the only one who would choose 'oddness' in preference to marriage. She is untouched by stereotypical feminine traits, and it has to be said, is not entirely likeable in her aggressive masculinity. The contrast we are offered is Mary Barfoot, of whom we are told, '... her abilities were of a kind uncommon in women, or at all events very rarely developed in one of her sex. She could have filled a place on a board of directors, have taken an active part in municipal government — nay, perchance in national. And this turn of intellect consisted with many traits of character so strongly feminine that people thought of her with as much tenderness as admiration'.[38] Inspite of her intellect, then, Mary Barfoot is an independent woman who does not threaten. Rhoda Nunn, by contrast, inspires admiration but little tenderness, and she herself displays none. She is brutally harsh in her treatment of the young woman who has 'defected' from the school and its precepts in becoming the mistress of a married man. Abandoned by her lover and destitute, Mary wishes to take her back, but Rhoda refuses, and the woman commits suicide.

Mary, unlike Rhoda, is a believer in love and marriage. She is altogether softer, more 'womanly' than Rhoda. Rhoda has no feminine traits. Gissing makes her masculine in physique and appearance. She had '... a vigorous frame' and a countenance which at first view '... seemed masculine, its expression somewhat aggressive', although with a hint of an underlying softness.[39] Her behaviour confirms her appearance, nowhere more so than in her stance towards other women. She has no confidantes, not even Mary. And when she suffers so miserably at Barfoot's hands, she does so alone. She offers a sharp contrast to Meredith's Diana who, when abandoned by Dacier, is brought back to life by the lover-like ministrations of her friend Emma. Rhoda overcomes her emotions in a bitter and solitary struggle. She bears her suffering 'like a man'. For having made Rhoda Everard Barfoot's equal, and given her stereotypically masculine traits, Meredith can, it seems, relate the two only through a plot structure based on contest. The struggle for domination which comprises their relationship resembles the zero-sum combat common to masculine genres such as the western and the crime-thriller. Usually the contestants represent good and evil, and occasionally the pair, equally matched, perish together. Sherlock Holmes and Moriarty disappeared over the cliff edge together, locked in mortal combat. (Holmes had to suffer resurrection by popular demand.) But the contest is usually an all-male affair, although an interesting comparison might be made with Wilkie Collins's *Woman in White*, where the more compelling pair of combatants are unquestionably not Walter Hartright and Sir Percival Glyde, but Marian and Count Fosco.

The object of the contest between Everard and Rhoda is identical for both; subjugation of the other: 'Loving her as he had never thought to love ... he could be satisfied with nothing short of unconditional surrender. Delighting in her independence of mind, he still desired to see her in complete subjugation to him. ...'[40] Rhoda initially does not wish to swerve from her chosen path of oddness. But she nevertheless wants the 'common triumph of her sex'. She wants to extract from him a proposal of marriage which she has no intention of accepting; to inspire in him a love which she will not reciprocate: 'She would not dismiss him peremptorily. He should prove the quality of his love. ... Coming so late, the experience must yield her all it had to yield of delight and contentment'.[41]

As each, against their intentions, becomes more seriously engrossed with the other, the game becomes real and the contest shifts its object. He wants her to accept the offer of a 'free union' which will not be a serious one. Once she has proved herself willing to accept him on these terms, he will marry her. She, on the other hand, will be satisfied only when she has brought him to the full offer of marriage. After their 'perfect day' in the lakes it is Rhoda who gains her point. But neither is satisfied. Each fears they have been exposed as weak. Moral victory finally belongs to Rhoda for when Everard returns to repeat his proposal, she unmasks the game he was playing with his first offer. This time she insists on a free union, which he cannot seriously contemplate. His bluff is called. Rhoda emerges as a strong and independent woman who has grown in stature and self-knowledge in true heroic fashion. She is the hero of the novel. Everard, diminished, retreats into a conventional marriage with the more pliantly feminine Agnes Brissenden.

If the problem with Meredith's *Diana of the Crossways* is that its resolution in Diana's second marriage to Redworth is a defeat of the heroine and everything she stands for, that of *The Odd Women* is that Rhoda's victory over Everard is an evasion of the problem posed by the novel — the basis on which a different type of relationship between the sexes might be created when the inequalities which women suffer are removed. When this problem is placed within a plot structure of contest, then the outcome is preordained as one which denies the possibility of any viable alternative to marriage based on inequality, domination and submission. The Rhoda-Everard story undermines the Monica-Widdowson-Bevis subplot and the novel's commitment to female independence. For if we take Rhoda to stand for the typical new woman and Everard for the typical intelligent male's response to her, then we can only conclude that there is no hope for a more equitable relationship between the sexes. The independent woman must remain celibate; a heroine who cannot mate. Rhoda's is a phyrric victory. For while Everard suffers moral defeat, his 'independence' ensures that the costs are small. He is free to marry Agnes. Rhoda returns to the status quo ante. The novel closes as it opened, with the Madden sisters still talking, with an optimism that we now know to be unfounded, of opening a school. In spite of Rhoda's effort to 'make her talk as inspiriting as ever' and to encourage the sisters to make of the dead Monica's child 'a brave woman', the novel's and Rhoda's last words strike a truer note: 'Poor little child'.[42] Rhoda's victory is remarkably like defeat.

6.
Nineteenth-Century Feminism and Fiction, II: The Woman's New Woman

How Different from us?

Miss Buss and Miss Beale
Cupid's darts do not feel.
How different from us
Miss Beale and Miss Buss.[1]

'I have ploughed, and planted, and gathered into barns and no man could head me! And ain't I a woman? I could work as much and eat as much as a man — when I could get it — and bear the lash as well! And ain't I a woman? I have born thirteen children and seen them most all sold off to slavery, and when I cried out with my mother's grief, none but Jesus heard me! And ain't I a woman?'[2]

Not surprisingly, for feminist writers of new woman fiction, the new woman had a different significance than she had for Gissing. But the new woman as she was constructed in fiction by both men and women, feminists and anti-feminists, moved within a common set of constraints, faced similar dilemmas.

The nineteenth-century women's movement, in fighting to improve the legal, political and social position of women, necessarily challenged prevailing socio-cultural definitions of femininity and masculinity. The gender order was placed under spotlights and a furious debate on what it meant to be a real man, a real woman, ensued. But we have seen that the meaning of femininity was on the whole and with important exceptions challenged only within limits which left its core intact. It was argued in chapter 5 above that this could be explained in part at least by the manner in which middle-class identity was bound up with prevailing constructions of femininity. Only a feminism which fought for the elimination of class oppression, could fight sex oppression without tying itself to the perpetuation of some aspects of conventional femininity. And even then it was difficult to avoid slipping into an image of 'woman' which was far more limited than the corresponding image of 'man'.

Sojourner Truth made her famous speech, quoted above, to the National Convention on Woman's Rights at Akron, Ohio, in 1851. It was a deeply moving and effective challenge to conventional definitions of gender as they were used to rationalize the subjection of women. More fundamentally it was a challenge to a white middle-class feminism which had mounted its campaigns with scant regard for the black and working-class women for whom prevailing definitions of femininity were a hollow mockery. The dubious privileges of women were claimed and allowed only on a strict basis of class and race. The rules of feminine propriety were only applied to white middle-class women. Slave women in the southern United States were subject to the full rigours of fieldwork, and its brutal discipline under the whip, on a basis of strict sex equality.[3] Portrayed as victims, like Harriet Beecher Stowe's Eliza, or Elizabeth Gaskell's Ruth, working-class women, black and white, American and British, could be sketched in a manner which fitted conventional definitions of femininity and were calculated to arouse compassion. The working-class sister as victim of male brutality, who wishes nothing better than to be permitted to be a true, womanly woman, is a familiar figure in nineteenth-century fiction. More rarely, a different picture is painted of strong, healthy women glorying in their strength.

Howard Munby had given us an unforgettable picture of Hannah Cullwick, and by encouraging her to keep her own diary for him, he secured for us Hannah's self-portrait, one of the few documents in which the voice of working-class women of the nineteenth century is heard.[4] And Angela Davis argues that the majority of enslaved women survived, and in the process acquired characteristics which women were supposed incapable of developing. She quotes a Mississippi traveller, impressed by the sight of '... forty of the largest and strongest women I ever saw together; they were all in a simple uniform dress of a bluish check stuff; their legs and feet were bare; they carried themselves loftily, each having a hoe over the shoulder, and walking with a free, powerful swing like chasseurs on the march'.[5] The very existence of such women threatened to break the necessary connection forged by ideologies of femininity between sex and gender. These women were doing and required to do things which were supposed to be beyond the capacity of their sex, yet the rhetorical force of Sojourner Truth's refrain, 'Ain't I a woman?' was difficult to gainsay.

However there is a key difference between the relationship of sex to gender in the case of women and of men as those relationships are typically constructed. Femininity in all its guises is much more narrowly defined than is masculinity, with a much more systematic attempt to link its defining characteristics to biological functions. In the late nineteenth century, femininity was positively defined in terms of a narrow set of attributes supposed to be natural to woman as a result of her reproductive and nurturing role. Because her maternal role required her to have an emotional attachment to her child, 'nature' had endowed her a general propensity to emotion, a general, altruistic responsiveness to others, and a capacity for suffering and self-sacrifice in the interests of those she loved. While the exact relationship of these qualities to the moral sense is unclear, a natural propensity to moral rectitude was also commonly attributed to women.

Masculinity, by contrast, was and remains an open-ended concept, defined in terms of acting in and on the world. While there is some attempt to explain man's propensity to action in terms of his sexual nature and his physical strength and energy, masculinity is not contained by biology and relationships as is femininity. Begetting children is neither a necessary nor sufficient condition of manliness, which has no single common denominator. A man may prove his manliness precisely by being different to other men, by raising himself above them in some way, mentally or physically. But sexuality and reproduction, together with emotional sensitivity and the capacity for self-sacrifice, are the bottom line in defining and proving womanhood. Sojourner Truth recognized this in making her rhetorical appeal as she did. It was her children, and her suffering as a mother when they were brutally sold from her which made her claim to womanhood unanswerable. But it is this claim which in turn reinforces the ideological bottom line. The father of children could never established an effective rhetoric of masculinity in the same terms.

The logic followed by Sojourner Truth was a socio-logic rather than one dictated absolutely by biology. This same socio-logic is to be found in the rules evolved in new woman fiction. Within its pages had to be determined what a woman might do and say and think while remaining respectable, a woman, and a heroine. Like Sojourner Truth, women might establish that they could do what men could do. Like her, they had to prove in addition, like today's female athletes, that they remained nonetheless 'real women'.

Because these heroines were middle-class, their 'masculine' capabilities were inevitably displayed by mental rather than physical attributes. A heroine who was literally strong might invite comparison not with men but with workers. Hence the recurrent figure in this fiction of the woman of 'genius'. The intellectually or artistically gifted woman proved that women might be the equal of men, and exposed the injustice of the inferior education they received, the lack of opportunities for developing those gifts. However the heroine-as-genius had a certain drawback from a didactic point of view. Precisely because she was a genius, she might be discounted as 'exceptional' and therefore as a poor argument for women in general. Hence the second obligation laid by their authors on these women: they had to demonstrate their common sisterhood with 'ordinary women'. They had to establish that, unlike Miss Buss and Miss Beale, they were no different from us. Unlike them, the woman's new woman was constrained to prove herself a real woman inspite of her genius.

But the ways in which this might be done were narrow, and returned the definition of woman back into the old groove. She might have a child to whom she gave a mother's love and sacrifice; she might fall in love, or inspire a great love; she might endure great deprivation and suffering for another. The vast majority of woman's new women did one or another of these things, and often all three. But the net effect of such plot resolutions was to backhandedly confirm what feminism denied: the naturalness of gender.

If the man's new woman usually suffered either the fate of Meredith's Diana — reduction to conventional womanliness, or that of Gissing's Rhoda — construction as essentially a man in a woman's body, that of the woman's new woman was to be a superwoman. The natural aristocrat of her sex by virtue of exceptional intellectual, artistic or spiritual qualities, she was often literally an aristocrat. Her name denoted her lofty character — Ideala (Sarah Grand's *Ideala*); Hadria, Algina (Mona Caird's *Daughters of Danaus*); Evadne, Angelica (Sarah Grand's *Heavenly Twins*). She was 'different from us', but not in the manner of Miss Buss and Miss Beale.

Domestic ideology, wedded to a form of social Darwinism, had been used to account for differences between women, especially differences of class and race. Sojourner Truth's and Hannah Cullwick's strong arm was explained in terms of an evolutionary scale in which the middle-class feminine ideal occupied a higher plane. As so often happened in the nineteenth-century women's movement, this notion was taken up and put to a new purpose — with the unfortunate effect of opening up feminism to some pretty dubious companions, such as eugenicism and racism.

Sarah Grand

Sarah Grand is prominent among the women who wrote new woman fiction in the eighteen-nineties and who subsequently 'disappeared'. She lived to a ripe old age, and was something of a celebrity in Bath where 'Madame Grand', as she styled herself, held the post of Mayoress from 1922-9. When she died in 1943, '... even her obiturists had to work hard to recall her'.[6] But her novel, *The Heavenly Twins*, published in 1893, had been a runaway best seller and was acclaimed as a work of genius by George Bernard Shaw.[7]

The Heavenly Twins is an extraordinary book which is unreadable today, and not simply by virtue of the fact that it is long since out of print. Kersley estimates that the book, sold initially to Heinemann for £100, earned royalties of almost £18,000 in total for its author.[8] It was reprinted six times within the first year of publication, and sold about 20,000 copies within two years. It was even more successful in the United States of America. Its successor, *The Beth Book* which appeared in 1897, was less well received and probably owed its success in large part to the reputation of the earlier work. Yet it was this latter novel that Virago chose to reissue in their Modern Classics series, not the more famous predecessor. Reading both books today, it can only be said that they made the right choice. *The Beth Book* has its longeurs, but also redeeming features in its account of Beth's childhood.

The Heavenly Twins is the ultimate big baggy monster. The novel runs to six books, in 679 closely printed pages. It consists of three plots; the story of the heroine Evadne's celibate marriage; of Angelica, one of the heavenly twins of the title, and her transvestite relationship with a tenor singer; and finally of Evadne's courtship and second marriage as told by her second husband. Unlike the orthodox multiple-plot Victorian novel, however, these three plots are not interwoven after the first part. Rather they are like separate novels end to end, with overlapping characters.

The sensation which *Heavenly Twins* occasioned was a function of its unprecedented daring in broaching in fiction the subject which had caused such scandal during the campaign for the repeal of the Contagious Diseases Act. The figure of 'the victim of matrimony' was a familiar one in fiction. Ann Brontë was one of many writers who had helped to develop this plot.[9] But Sarah Grand added a new dimension of horror and urgency in her portrayal of this newly acknowledged threat to the ignorant/innocent bride. To brute insensitivity, drunkenness, dissolution and violence, all already familiar, was added that of the incurable disease which might be passed on to wives and children.

Evadne, the heroine, escapes this fate because she is knowledgeable above the norm for a secluded young girl. She is intellectually curious and has read many volumes of natural and medical science found fortuitously in the attic. So when, on her marriage to Colonel Colquhoun, she learns through a letter of his dissolute past, her fear of the physically damaging consequences as well as her moral outrage leads her to refuse to consummate the marriage. Her friend Edith, who marries a brother officer of Colquhoun's is not so lucky, and it was the account of Edith's syphilitic child and her own death from dementia which caused so much scandal when the novel appeared.

The horror generated by this theme is not contained within the predominantly realist conventions of the novel but spills out into gothic moments. There is one scene which could have come straight from the pages of *Mysteries of Udolpho*. An elderly, reformed aristocratic rake and his beautiful daughter, the bountiful Lady Fulda, converts to Rome, have both experienced the same vision, a smiling child who appears from time to time on a panel in the chapel of the Duke's palace. It is decided that the panel must be removed, and the spirit laid with due ritual, by a team of priests, at midnight. Nature obliges with an appropriate wild storm and the panel is removed to reveal what appears to be the body of a child but proves to be a battered wax doll. We are left with no definite explanation of either the doll's burial, or the vision. Possibly the first may have been another one of the heavenly twin's 'pranks' — but possibly not.

The horror is repeated in the final story narrated by Evadne's second husband. On discovering that she is pregnant, Evadne attempts to kill herself out of a morbid fear that her child, too, may prove to have some hereditary taint.

Angelica's story is mainly contained in books IV and V, although the story of her and her twin brother's childhood has interlarded the first half of the novel which is primarily devoted to Evadne's marriage and Edith's story. The twins were variously regarded as tiresome or entertaining by contemporary critics, and are usually described as providing a sugar coating which would keep the mass of readers going and make more palatable the bitter pill of moral purpose contained in the Evadne sections of the novel. Grand draws on the popular view of twins as interchangeable in order to give plausibility to their childhood and its legacy of near androgyny. At Evadne's wedding, bridesmaid and page change clothes. On approaching adolescence, they jointly refuse to be taught separately and insist on a common programme of learning. But the reckoning comes for Angelica as she begins to feel the conflicting emotions of adolescence, and to recognize the constraints of femininity and domesticity, the lack of outlets for her energy and her musical intellect. Traumatized by the sight of Edith's syphilitic child, she proposes to a man twenty years older than her on condition that she may do as she likes.

We are taken thus far with Angelica's story as it is interlarded with Evadne's, without learning whether Mr Kilroy accepts her proposal and its terms. Book IV, in which she is placed at the centre, is entitled 'The Tenor and the Boy — an Interlude'. We do not learn the identity of the 'boy' until the last few pages of Book IV, when it is revealed to the reader and at the same time to the tenor, that the boy he has befriended is actually the girl he has idealized without ever speaking to her, and with whom he has fallen in love; also that the girl is a married woman. Angelica destroys the idealized

angel with whom he had fallen in love, by revealing the reality of
the tomboy behind the image of femininity. And she destroys the
masculine friend, by revealing the girl behind the assumed clothing. She has adopted the disguise in recognition that, childhood
past, the only scope for resisting domestic femininity is in this
guise: 'The charm ... has all been in the delight of associating
with a man intimately who did not know I was a woman. ...
Had you known that I was a woman — even you — the pleasure
would have been spoilt for me. ... Your manner to me has been
quite different from that of any other man I ever knew. Some
have fawned on me, degrading me with the supposition that I
exist for the benefit of man alone, and that it will gratify me
above all else to know that I please him; and some few, such as
yourself, have embarrassed me by putting me on a pedestal,
which is, I can assure you, an exceedingly cramped and uncomfortable position ... with you alone of all men ... I almost think I
have been on an equal footing. ...'[10]

The novel leaves an impression of bleak pessimism in spite of
its femininism and in this it is not uncharacteristic. Mona Caird's
most popular feminist novel, *Daughters of Danaus*, shares pessimism to an even greater degree, as does Mary Cholmondeley's
Red Pottage.[11] Grand was heavily influenced by the doctrine of
evolution as it had been applied to social development. She had
added the doctrine, taken from domestic ideology itself, of the
moral superiority of women, and cast it in terms of evolutionary
theory. The survival of the race depended on animal instincts
which were held to be stronger in men than in women. But if
these instincts were allowed free reign, unrestrained by moral
control, the result would be not evolutionary progress but 'race
degeneracy'. The sex which by 'nature' held the greatest moral
power, was typically kept in ignorance and seclusion, like Edith
had been; the sex with the stronger animal impulse had the
social power to indulge it unrestrained, yet was encouraged to
mate subsequently with disastrous consequences.

At this turning point, with the 'advanced races' poised
between higher evolutionary progress and degeneracy, the fate
of 'the race' Grand held, lay with women. This hope is expressed
in the novel by a minor character, an American, who is one of a
number of 'new men' who form a kind of chorus throughout the
novel, commenting from time to time on the position of woman,
her oppression, and her capacities: 'Ah, these are critical times,

but I believe ... that the women will save us. I do not fear the fate of the older peoples. I am sure that we shall not fall into nothingness from the present height of our civilization, by reason of our sensuality and vice, as all the great nations have done heretofore. The women will rebel. The women will not allow it. ...'[12]

But the optimism expressed by such 'advanced' individuals is not echoed in plot outcomes. Angelica, in spite of her marital compact which permits her unlimited freedom, respects her husband's horror that she will become a professional musician. She is left at the close of the novel with no outlet for her energy, in an admittedly unconventional marriage with a man whom she refers to as 'Daddy'. Evadne's intellectual gifts are equally thwarted and she retains a precarious hold on her sanity by carefully avoiding sight and knowledge of evil. Mona Caird's Hadria, like most of the new women a genius with the potential to become a great composer, finds it impossible to free herself from the demands of an ailing mother, and like the heroine of Radclyffe Hall's *The Unlit Lamp*, lives to see the loss of her powers. But it is Mary Cholmondeley who produces the most vivid and savage image of defeat. Her heroine, Hester, has her 'child', the manuscript of a book lovingly created at great cost to health and under the most adverse domestic circumstances, deliberately destroyed by fire by a morally outraged brother.

The Beth Book is an exception in offering us a heroine-genius who manages not only to escape from her appalling marriage, but also to survive, mentally and physically unscathed, to be a successful writer and public speaker. *The Beth Book* is subtitled 'Being a Study of the Life of Elizabeth Caldwell Maclure, a Woman of Genius'. It is a species of biographical fiction, structured around a life, although it terminates with maturity, literary success and love, rather than with death. As the subtitle informs us, it is the life of an exceptional woman, a 'woman of genius'. The bulk of the book, and its best passages, deals with the childhood of the heroine. The book opens with earliest childhood memories; remembered fragments of the pre-verbal infant in snapshot scenes. No ordinary child this, but a budding genius, we are party to the development of her extraordinary sensibility. We are shown the six-year old explaining to her wondering father how she has learnt to 'sing' her awareness of natural beauty into poetry:

'What other "things like that" do you know, Beth?'
'The song of the sea in the shell,
    The swish of the grass in the breeze,
The sound of the faraway bell,
    The whispereing leaves on the trees,'

Beth burst out instantly.

'Who taught you that, Beth?' her father asked.
'Oh, no one taught me, papa,' she answered. 'It just came to me —/.
...'[13]

And Beth goes on to explain just how the sounds suggested the
words, and how she explored the various patterns she could
make with them. For Beth's 'genius', culminating in a successful
career, is largely untutored. It is her brothers who are sent away
to school. Beth is (badly) taught at home by her mother, and
receives only two years' formal schooling. In fact her whole
upbringing is chaotic. Her moral sensibility is schooled by her
Great Aunt Victoria under whose influence Beth falls for only a
few short months. Apart from this one relative, Beth's only tutor
would appear to be the natural and social environment in which
she is allowed to wander freely and her own keen observation of
its properties. So that although the book is a passionate plea for
a sound moral and intellectual training for children in general
and girls in particular, Beth's own story rather suggests that
genius will out, whatever you do to it!

If the dominant figure in the book is 'the childhood of genius'
the second is the equally familiar 'victim of matrimony'. Two-
thirds of the way through the novel, Beth marries, at the age of
sixteen, an older man who is a doctor and we see her childhood
sensitivity brutally trampled on in a marriage which is degrading
and defiling. Her husband is revealed to be a sadist as well as a
sensualist. He is employed in the local Lock hospital and in his
spare time and for his own pleasure, as well as for profit,
practices vivisection at home on stray dogs. Beth is introduced to
women active in the women's movement. She leaves her husband and takes an attic room in London where, in isolation, she
writes her books, nurses a young fellow lodger, and finally falls
ill herself from cold and near starvation, unaware that her book
has sold and that she has become rich by virtue of the recovery
of her Great Aunt Victoria's investments.

I have said that new women heroines had to prove that they shared their common femininity with their ordinary sisters, in spite of being exceptional women of genius. This is not quite right. If we divide conventional femininity into its positive and negative attributes, then the new women display only the former while 'ordinary women' tend to display more of the latter. They are vain, treacherous, trivial. But in our heroine, the positive virtues of femininity are displayed to excess, her great moral sensibility and her selflessness. She sacrifices herself to keep the sick lodger supplied with food and coal, which she herself carries up several flights of stairs. She in her own attic goes without. She sells her best clothes, and when these are gone, sacrifices her hair which she sells for a wig. But she reveals nothing of the real state of affairs to the sick lodger, even humbly accepting his reproaches over her shorn locks.

The Beth Book is narrated in the third person by a narrator whose identity is not disclosed. But the most plausible position which can be imputed to her is that of an older Beth looking back and describing her past life as is the convention in much biographical fiction. But such fiction is usually written in the first person. Grand's use of the third person may have been intended to prevent the reader from making this imputation about the narrator. Sarah Grand denied that the book was autobiographical yet she established no distance, save that of the impersonal voice, between imputed author, narrator, and character. It is a book which is difficult not to read as autobiography as there is so much to identify Beth McClure with Frances McFall (Sarah Grand's married name). Her biographer, Gillian Kersley, simply assumes that Beth is her author in childhood. Where she lacks direct evidence about that childhood, she quotes freely from *The Beth Book*, substituting for the character's first name, that of the author.[14]

Read as autobiography the book can seem monstrously egotistical. Speaking of Beth's mother, the narrator tells us, 'She could not have been made to comprehend that Beth, a girl, was the one member of the family who deserved a good chance, the only one for whom it would have repaid her to produce extra advantages',[15] and the book is littered with such judgements of Beth's superiority and of the inferiority of sisters, brothers, mother, husband. It is only necessary to substitute 'I' for 'she' in such passages to see how insufferable it would be written in the first person. The fiction must be maintained that the narrator is *not* talking about herself.

However, the effect of third person narration is curious. Modleski uses Berger[16] and Barthes[17] to analyse the use of third person narration in Harlequin romances.[18] It allows the reader to place herself in the position of the heroine and to watch herself being looked at without destroying the illusion that the heroine is unconscious of the look. *The Beth Book* produces a somewhat similar effect. Yet since intellect in a heroine can be displayed, the use of a narrator to underline and assert it is at best heavy-handed.

Literary Survival Value

If we ask why *The Beth Book, The Heavenly Twins, The Daughters of Danaus* and much other popular feminist fiction of the time did not survive into the annals of 'literature' the answer might seem to be simple. They were didactic and polemical books whose popularity was a function of their time. *The Heavenly Twins* was offered to a number of publishers before it found one ready to risk publication and it is interesting to see the reasons for its rejection. Some feared that it would offend. Kersley quotes one publisher as having written: 'We do not say that the ideals you employ are coarse, though we have no doubt critics will be less scrupulous, but we venture to assert that they are antagonistic to all culture and refinement. ... All delicately-minded women must feel themselves aggrieved, if not insulted, by the prominence which is given to the physical side of marriage. ... Even had I not the traditions of my House to go by in the case of *The Heavenly Twins*, I could not, and would not dare to place your work in the way of ladies, who compose so large a proportion of the novel-reading public'.[19] Clearly this publisher miscalculated and a taboo, once lifted, may for that very reason excite tremendous interest. The book's enormous popularity may have been the result of the timely flouting of the very taboo which almost had resulted in its failure to find a publisher.

But Meredith, for Chapmans, rejected it on different grounds. He made a gross error, and not his first, from the point of view of the firm as a profit-making enterprise. However reading the book today, it is hard not to concur with his judgement: 'Evadne would kill a better work with her heaviness. ... The writer should be advised to put this manuscript aside until she has got the art of driving a story'.[20] *The Beth Book*, riding on the reputation of the earlier success, received less critical acclaim. The qualities of the early chapters on Beth's childhood were rightly acknowledged. But Frank Harris's objection to its 'egotistical outpourings'[21] is one which the work invites. We do not have to suppose a male conspiracy to account for the disappearance of these books.

However there were other women writers of new woman fiction whose contemporary success might have occurred independently of the furore which surrounded this type of fiction — for example, Olive Schreiner, George Egerton and Mary Cholmondeley. Of the three, only Cholmondeley wrote a great deal of fiction. Schreiner had completed *The Story of an African Farm* when she arrived in England at the age of twenty-six in 1881. It was published in 1883 by Chapmans on Meredith's recommendation, and was given a tremendous reception. But she never completed another novel of substance. *From Man to Man* was the subject of continuous revision and redrafting until her death when it remained unfinished.[22] George Egerton's *Keynotes* was published in 1893.[23] She contributed to the first volume of *The Yellow Book* and was acclaimed among the fin de siècle intelligentsia. But her talent was for short stories, and writers who wrote only short stories rarely found a place in the literary canon.

Mary Cholmondeley's literary idol was George Eliot and inevitably, when her work is compared to Eliot's, she is found wanting. One irony of the situation of women writers is the manner in which the few great writers admitted to the canon have been used as sticks to beat the rest. But when *Red Pottage* is compared with novels written by contemporary writers such as Meredith or Gissing who made it, so to speak, into the second eleven but never quite beyond that point,[24] it stands up in my view very well. Like Meredith, Cholmondeley has an acid wit and her book is very funny in spite of also being very bitter. Why did this immensely popular and critically acclaimed book not survive any better than Sarah Grand's didactic fiction?

It is not possible to offer definite explanations but conspiracy theory will not answer. Rather we may look on literary survival in terms of loosely defined rules or codes, which have tended to work against women. Firstly, it is authors rather than books that survive, with a few notable exceptions such as *Wuthering Heights*. It is the *auteur* who is constructed in literary criticism rather than the text. A single text is seldom enough to establish that status. Once it is established however, *all* the author's texts become worthy of study however flawed any particular one may be, just as all the paintings of a 'great master' will command aesthetic interest and a high price. Writers who, for whatever reason, have a small output will be at a disadvantage. Yet we have seen that women in the nineteenth century typically began their literary apprenticeships later in life than their male colleagues. If and insofar as they were also encumbered with pressing domestic duties, they would have been additionally handicapped.

Secondly, polemical writings usually do not last beyond the moment of controversy. Whenever the 'woman question' is raised, then feminist fiction will be written and earlier feminist fiction rediscovered. Whether or not feminist fiction is always and necessarily tendentious, it will tend to be seen as such when feminism is out of fashion. Books by women which foreground the woman question are likely to be so labelled whatever their literary merits may be. *Red Pottage* may have been a victim of this kind of labelling since, unlike *Daughters of Danaus* or *The Heavenly Twins*, it is not didactic. But it was the only one of Mary Cholmondeley's novels which attracted much notice.

Thirdly, woman-to-woman fiction is coded out of 'literature'. While feminist fiction in the eighteen-nineties was widely read and was not necessarily addressed exclusively to women, women were the preferred readers. Woman-to-woman forms are not permitted to become part of the general stock of 'cultural capital'.

The male producers of new woman fiction, with the exception of Grant Allen, did not fall foul of any of these unwritten rules. A man writing such fiction is not open to the charge of tendentiousness to the same extent as is a woman. He can claim to be disinterested if his fiction seems to support the cause of feminism. But in any case Hardy, Gissing and Meredith did not only write new woman fiction, and they wrote extensively. Their work has survived to become part of the publicly recognized stock of cultural capital. But while the bulk of that capital is male-produced, women play a major role in its transmission from generation to generation.

7.
Education and the Transmission of a Literary Culture

As English literature began to find a place within the curriculum, especially at higher levels of the education system, a new dimension was added to the institutional structure within which literary production and consumption were organized. The study of English placed English literature within the orbit of one of the major ideological institutions of capitalism, one which, unlike publishing and the commercial libraries, was not directly subject to market forces. The educational institutionalization of English modified to some extent the effects of the transformation of literature into a commodity. Its ideological effects were mediated by formal study rather than informal entertainment. Women continued to play a key role in the transmission of the literary culture in schools and colleges. For the entry of English onto the university curriculum was coterminous with the entry of women into higher education. And the subject which they chose above all others to study was the new discipline of English, alongside modern languages.

English Literature in the University: the Commodity Transformed

English literature was taught as part of the London BA from 1850 and found a place on the syllabus at various provincial universities during the course of the second half of the century — at Manchester in 1850, Leeds in 1874, Birmingham in 1880, and

Liverpool and Nottingham in 1881. But it is Oxbridge which confers cultural legitimacy and Oxbridge withheld paternal recognition until the twentieth century. The story of the fortunes of English at Oxford and more particularly, Cambridge, has been told before and need not detain us here.[1]

English literature when it began to be taught in schools and colleges stimulated market demand on a new basis. It might have had more impact than it did, however, because of certain peculiarities in the way in which it was adopted. Firstly, it was constituted at the university, though not in schools, as literary criticism rather than creative writing. In Britain, creative writing courses have never achieved the same curricular presence which they have in the United States. Secondly, higher education in this country even in the period of expansion, post-Robbins, never reached anything like the proportion of the people which was served in the States. With a population approximately four times the size of the United Kingdom, the college population of the United States has been estimated as ten times larger. And finally 'Our English professors ... prefer their literature cold and clear and very dead'.[2] Nevertheless in spite of these limits, the expansion of education in the twentieth century and the establishment of English on the curriculum created a vast and lucrative market for literature which changed the nature of the literary market-place.

Literary criticism has often been seen as an activity parasitical upon the production of the literary text. But it has been argued that it is rather that activity which constitutes literature by determining what will count as a literary text.[3] The authoritative journal, alongside the university syllabus, is the major constituting instrument. But here, too, the university is crucial because it is those journals which are closely connected with the university which tend to gain recognition. The journals are dominated by academics and since the second world war so too is reviewing in the national press.

The proportion of living literature studied in universities and schools is small, so producers of literary fiction depend on the journals and reviews to establish their claims to this status rather than on inclusion within the syllabus. Yet until the text is established as an object of study its status as literature is insecure. The belated recognition of the contribution of the novel to English literature did not therefore release contemporary novelists from the exigencies of production for a general market. However there was a gradual differentiation within the production of fiction between those who are contestants for the prize of critical recognition, whose work is to be the object of critical study, and those entered in a different contest, the would-be best-seller. Both are of course producers of commodities but of different kinds. The best-seller remains under the primary obligation to entertain through the production of engrossing narratives. The greatest possible number of readers must be persuaded to buy. Literary fiction has on occasion hit the best-seller list. Some twentieth-century novelists whose fiction has sold in millions but whose work has gained a place in the corpus of literature include Iris Murdoch, Doris Lessing, Margaret Drabble, Alan Sillitoe, John Fowles and William Golding to name but a few. However as argued in chapter 4, the relationship between literature and popular sales was and remains problematic. For literary works the first target is critical acclaim which as we have seen may actually be placed in jeopardy by too great a degree of popularity in the first instance. Once they have attained this status however, then sales may reach astronomical proportions as texts gain a secure place on the syllabus and become required reading for successive generations of students. Books such as Sillitoe's *Loneliness of the Long Distance Runner*, or Golding's *Lord of the Flies*, owe their sales as much to their being taken up as school texts as to their ability to entertain.

However this process does not often help the living author because of the tendency to elevate only dead texts. Nineteenth-century 'classics' have been given a new lease of life by the development of literature in education. Probably few nineteenth-century novels would survive to be read today were it not for this market. Jane Austen, certainly; her unfinished *Sanditon*, published in 1975 with an ending written by 'Another Lady', dominated the bestseller list selling 22,000 in hardback in the first ten weeks.[4] And Dickens, too, would sell without much doubt. The enormous popularity of the literary adaptation on film and especially television might secure the survival of many more but it is difficult to determine how far this is in turn parasitical upon the English curriculum in schools. Objects of entertainment at the moment of their production, these works have survived by becoming primarily objects of study. Their sales today do not depend on their capacity still to please. Their market is guaranteed simply by their inclusion on the syllabus.

Indirectly the renewed sales of nineteenth-century fiction in cheap reprints may have aided the fortunes of the literary novel today by providing a staple source of revenue for literary publishers for whom they have always been a major source of income. Chapmans prospered year in, year out, on the strength of Dickens' reprints.[5] Such publishers can afford to launch new writers of promise and in so doing may enhance their own reputation as *literary* publishers.[6]

Nevertheless the literary novel survives on the margins of commercial publication and is only rarely in its own right a financial proposition which secures a reasonable livelihood for its producer.[7] We are subject, periodically, to gloomy forecasts of its imminent death. But the institutionalization of English has aided the literary author in another way. Typically the author's royalties were, in the nineteenth century and today, supplemented by other kinds of work which a literary reputation might secure. Meredith and Jewsbury were publishers' readers, and most novelists wrote reviews and articles for the journals. The institutionalization of English added a further source of related income through teaching. Gissing wrote his *New Grub Street* at the point in time when the conditions of literary production under which his hero suffered, and which literally killed both Reardon and Biffen, were undergoing changes which would have smoothed their paths. A few years later, Reardon would have found a comfortable niche teaching literature in some obscure public or grammar school and he could have slowed down his literary output to suit his natural pace.[8]

'Live' literary fiction may on occasion hit the jackpot. But its survival does not depend on mass sales, and unlike the fiction produced for the best seller market, it is released from the requirement that it provide readily accessible entertainment. The institutionalization of English was certainly not responsible for the emergence of non-realist, experimental fictional forms at the end of the nineteenth and the beginning of the twentieth centuries. But the academy has protected and reproduced literary modernism and experimentation in more ways than one.

While it was the 'great tradition' which was overwhelmingly constituted as literature in schools and colleges once the novel became an object of such study and while it was initially poetry and then drama, rather than the novel, that was studied, nevertheless the institutionalization of English studies generated an essential component of the literary market, a pool of competent readers. Producers of the literary novel are participants in one of Becker's 'art worlds' which contain among their members not only the producers but also the suitably trained recipients. The competent readership for the contemporary novel as literature is supplied above all by students who have specialized in the study of English in schools and colleges.

The Entry of Women into Higher Education

As we have seen, the demand for improved educational opportunities for women was absolutely central to the women's movement in the nineteenth century. It provoked the most resistance where women competed directly with men. The line of least resistance was more often followed however, bringing women into disciplines and occupations, notably teaching, in which they had already established a foothold.

The connection between the movement for the improvement of women's education, and the teaching profession, is clear from the start. The first college for women was Queen's College, London, which was set up in 1848 for the purpose of improving the qualifications of governesses.[9] The women's colleges at Oxford and Cambridge which were established later in the century turned out large numbers of teachers. Over half the early Oxbridge female students became teachers and almost all the headteachers of the reformed Girls' Public Schools by the eighteen-nineties were Oxbridge trained. Pedersen notes the narrow social background of Oxbridge women. The vast majority were daughters of Gramscian traditional intellectuals, and relatively few the daughters of businessmen — 64 and 25 per cent respectively.

The entry of women into higher education was obstructed and resisted for decades. It entailed a restructuring of an ideology coordinated on strongly marked gender differences. The education of women was hotly debated within the terms of Victorian domestic ideology and the place of women in society, and it is rightly seen in the context of the history of nineteenth-century feminism for it required a determined feminist initiative to see it through. It must also be placed within its class and ideological context. It was part of a broad rethinking of bourgeois and working-class educational standards in the face of changes in the nature of capitalism, and of the extension of the franchise to working men. The exposure of the working class to the civilizing effects of high culture might be hoped, by the more progressive elements such as Arnold at least, to temper working-class radicalism and to mitigate the class struggle.[10] However it might less conveniently remove the rationale for class difference itself, the alleged 'natural' superiority of dominant over dominated, masters over men. In the context of the 1867 Reform Bill, Robert Lowe, one of the educational reformers who favoured the study of English, told the House of Commons, 'you should prevail upon our future masters to learn their letters'.[11]

But if the working class was to become educated, then it was even more urgent that intellectual class differentials should be maintained and the education of the bourgeoisie be reformed as well. The provision of education for the proletariat provoked a crisis in the education of bourgeois sons and daughters, the context of the 'great debate' described by Mathieson.[12] The systematic education of daughters outside the bourgeois home was new and revolutionary insofar as it opened up prospects for some women of independence and a viable alternative to marriage. It was also a necessary corollary of changes in the capitalist society of which it was a part. Women were about to be induced into the workforce in roles hitherto reserved for men, with the huge expansion of the tertiary sector so characteristic of the late nineteenth and twentieth centuries.[13] Clerical work, teaching, and a host of other occupations were about to take off on an unprecedented scale and were to draw on the labour of women. Such change inevitably provoked moral panic. But the most scurrilous resistance to the education of women occurred where they were seen to be entering into competition with their brothers for more lucrative spoils, in such professions as medicine.[14]

In the main however women were not competing but were being educated for occupations which were either new or which were rapidly feminized; occupations moreover which were readily reconciled with women's traditional family roles. Recent work on educational reforms for women in the nineteenth century emphasize, unlike the earlier literature, the continuities with prevailing definitions of the woman's role.[15] The functions to be performed by bourgeois women were traditional ones carried out under new circumstances which required a rather better educational training. Delamont argues that a condition of the success of the movement for the education of women was the support of bourgeois parents, a willingness on their part to educate their daughters at considerable expense. That support would not have been forthcoming had the parents believed that such education was incompatible with their traditional role as wives and mothers, or even that that education might open up attractive alternatives to this traditional role.[16] The education of girls began to be seen as a proper and necessary preparation for marriage and motherhood, not as an escape from it.

Gender and English

If women have provided the bulk of literature students, then it is equally true that the literature they have studied was and is male-produced and male-controlled within the literary critical establishment in spite of the honourable place within it attained by a handful of women novelists. Poetry and drama, the senior forms within the corpus, have yielded even fewer women whose texts have successfully passed through the filter of criticism to become 'literature'. The great tradition is humanist, and as such positively saturated with what Dale Spender has called 'he/man language'.[37] It is a tradition which claims to transcend divisions of class and sex to attain and articulate a true species-universality. However Spender goes on to argue that it carries the covert assumption that the male of the species defines normality, and the female some deviation or falling away. Women's texts may be admitted, provided they are not read as *women's* texts. Outside of a feminist context, any reference to the sex of Austen or Brontë will almost certainly be disparaging, linked to the exposure of weaknesses or limitations rather than to literary strengths. Even Virginia Woolf gets caught in this logic when she argues in *A Room of One's Own* for the essential androgyny of great literature. The great woman writer, she argues, must forget her sex and its grievances. But if Spender is right, the 'human' is only formally gender-neutral. Behind the apparent sexlessness we image a man. Androgynous greatness denies a woman her sex while it confirms the man's.[18]

If the literature constituted through the grid of criticism is primarily male produced and normatively masculine, the same is equally true of the chief actors within the critical grid in departments of English in the university and in the prestigious literary journals. It is interesting in this context to note the double marginalization suffered by Q.D. Leavis in relation to the Cambridge English School but also to a degree on *Scrutiny*. Mulhern notes that Q.D. Leavis, 'In practice [F.R.] Leavis's main collaborator; . . .' was 'never accorded the formal editorial status that was her due'.[19]

However it has been argued elsewhere[20] that the social activity of writing and criticism is, within British culture, gender-ambiguous. Gender as it is deployed in that culture can be used in relative as well as absolute terms. The gender attributes of a social role or activity will be more or less marked as masculine or feminine, depending on the comparative context. This can be seen in the case of social class. One motif which runs through cultural images of class locates the male working class as absolutely masculine, to uncivilized excess, while on the other hand, images of the effete and decadent upper class male abound. The bourgeois male appears as relatively civilized and 'softened' when compared to his working-class counterpart, refreshingly 'manly' when viewed in relation to the other end of the class spectrum. In bourgeois culture the bourgeois male marks the position of human normality. The worker is too masculine, the aristocrat not masculine enough, civilized to preciosity. In fact human manliness has a similar flavour of androgyny to that of the humanist culture, although needless to say only males may legitimately aspire to the status.

In spite of the manliness stridently claimed for its stock in trade by the literary critical establishment, literary criticism and the production of literature occupies, along with modern languages, the feminine polarity within the gender-order of the school and university curriculum. The masculine status of the physical sciences, like that of the working-class male, provides the undisputed limiting case. Science's self-image and the image it commands at large is replete with paradigmatically masculine attributes. It has effectively come to define in its methodology that most masculine virtue, rationality. But like the male working class, it is open to the suggestion that it is too grossly masculine. The fully rounded human being, claimed persistently as the product of the study of the humanities, is the male civilized, and to that degree, feminized. It is this claim which English has so successfully staked as its raison d'etre which has brought literature and literary criticism so perilously close to femininity. The manly human being is the product of the civilizing feminine upon the more brutal masculine. The arts, and English literary study in particular, have laid claim to a certain moral and cultural superiority which is at the same time a subtle and covert mark of inferiority. The logic is identical to that which structured nineteenth-century domestic ideology. Women were seen as both physically and intellectually inferior to men but morally superior. Compare the prevalent myths surrounding science and English in the school culture; maths and physics are consistently presented as more intellectually demanding, technical and difficult than English. In revealing metaphor, English, the arts and social studies are described as 'soft options'. Yet at the same time scientists and mathematicians carry the stereotype of being culturally and socially less sensitive and discriminating. The moral and social virtues are claimed by and accorded to the one as readily as the intellectual virtues to the other.

An identical 'civilizing power' is attributed to literature and to women. The striking similarity with which their ideal virtues have been described was in evidence before the period in which English gained its place upon the curriculum. It is clear in the nineteenth-century social problem novel. The civilizing influence of women and literature was to operate beneficially on masters and men and upon the relationship between them. The influence of women and literature might, it was hoped, temper the militant class antagonism of the one and the unfeeling utilitarianism of the other. The narratives of Elizabeth Gaskell's Manchester novels are structured around this hope. John Barton in *Mary Barton* and Frederick Thornton in *North and South*, are worker and master respectively, each in crisis and on course for disaster as they become locked in class conflict in the context of economic slump. Barton is fatally attracted to chartism and political violence; Thornton is proudly insensitive to the suffering of his starving and desperate workforce. The outcome in each case is foreshadowed by the relative immunity or lack of immunity of each man by virtue of his exposure to the dual civilizing influences. Thornton has a solid foundation laid by his part-time study of the classics — a pursuit frowned upon by his rigidly puritanical mother as unmanly and inappropriate to his class and occupation. His redemption is secured through the agency of a good womanly woman, Margaret Hale, whose love is instrumental in bringing Thornton to realize the need to modify his harsh utilitarian relationship to his workers and to show a more acceptable and human face to capitalism.[21]

The working man, John Barton, has no such luck. His author tells us 'The actions of the uneducated seem to me typified in those of Frankenstein, that master of many human qualities, ungifted with a soul. . . .'[22] Without exposure to literature because of his lack of education, Barton is also without a good woman. His wife dies early in the narrative, on which we are told, 'One of the good influences over John Barton . . . one of the ties which bound him down to the gentle humanities of the earth . . .' was lost.[23] Job Legh, another worker in the same novel, provides an interesting counter-example. He is able to refuse class militancy because of his induction into the humanizing values of knowledge afforded in this case by his amateur study of botany and by the influence of his musically gifted daughter, the blind Margaret. In another social problem novel of the same period, *Shirley*, Robert Moore's resolute resistance to feminine influence is weakened in an early scene in which Caroline corrects and reinterprets Robert's reading of *Coriolanus*.[24]

However belief in the humanizing effect of great literature, mobilized so effectively in the interests of gaining a place for English studies on the curriculum, has a certain uncomfortable logic in the era of specialization, an era coterminous with the period in which English staked its claim. In the mid-nineteenth century no hard and fast distinction was drawn, and similar claims might be and were staked for the humanizing effect of the study of natural science. Mathieson describes the 'great debate' over the curriculum which took place in the 1860s[25] and which was to a large extent a debate over the rival claims of English and natural science to replace classical studies as the humanizing element of a liberal education. Matthew Arnold championed English, Thomas Huxley the physical sciences. In the long run English had the advantage because a humanizing study must remain accessible outside a narrow circle of professional specialists and with the progress of science the latter soon ceased to be so. In the mid-nineteenth century the scholar-gentleman might reasonably hope to keep himself informed in the sciences as well as in literature and the arts and even to turn his hand to both. George Henry Lewes, like many of his circle, moved freely between the two.[26] While science in Britain was to some extent to remain the preserve of the brilliant amateur right up to the period of the second world war, the distance between scientific research and what could be transmitted in the school curriculum or in popular form grew increasingly great.

A second factor limited the claim of science to this general humanizing role. Such a claim necessarily hinged on the development of the subject at lower levels of the education system, in the schools where it might structure secondary socialization and character formation of pupils whether or not they were going on to study the subject professionally or at higher levels. For this a large number of teachers was required. But 'If you want science you must begin by creating science teachers'.[27] While the prevalent educational practices generated an abundant supply of teachers of classics, the same was never to be true of the natural sciences. Mulhern records that as late as 1919-20 the sciences, pure and applied, attracted only 33 per cent of university entrants, a proportion which had fallen to 26 per cent by 1929-30.[28] Moreover science degrees opened onto a number of careers more lucrative than teaching. The great advantage of both classics and English from this point of view was precisely their lack of vocational relevance outside of teaching. Finally, English could draw on a huge reservoir of students and teachers in the young women who, when given access to improved secondary and higher education, chose to study this new subject or were offered little alternative.

While the Leavisites broke decisively with the tradition of the amateur scholar/gentleman, as Mulhern has documented, drawing instead on recruits from the ranks of the petty bourgeoisie in search of a professional career and insisting on the need for scholarly rigour, it could not entirely escape the double-bind of professionalism and the claim to exercise a general humanizing effect. A discipline whose rationale even at the highest reaches of scholarship remained its humanizing capacity, was at odds with its own professionalization and always prone to incur the contemptuous dismissal of those who felt inclined to dispute what were considered its more arrogant claims. English studies at the university were and remained open to such sniping on the grounds that they were not constitutive of any real discipline. V.W. Robson, in the 1956 F.R. Leavis lecture, recalled being told by a classics don that English was a subject that an intelligent man could read in his bath.[29]

An interesting aspect of the battle of words over the establishment of English on the university curriculum is the way in which the claim to paradigmatically feminine virtues made on its behalf by supporters was countered with compelling logic by its detractors with accusations of equally stereotypical feminine vices. Without drawing attention to the way in which feminine stereotypes were in play, Baldick gives some good examples of this strategy: 'E.A. Freeman, the Regius Professor of History, predicted that the study of English would degenerate into mere "chatter about Shelley ... we do not want, we will not say frivolous subjects, but subjects which are merely light, elegant, interesting"'.[30] 'Colling ... was well aware, and very critical, of the tendencies towards mere gossip in literary studies'.[31] Later Baldick notes the fears of working men, recorded by Newbolt, that literature was 'merely ... an ornament, a polite accomplishment, a subject to be despised by really virile men'.[32] Mulhern provides another gem, this time from F.L. Lucas's virulent attack on English literature in 1932: 'as an education, Classics was peerless: "the study of its two literatures is saved from the effeminacy of many aesthetic pursuits by its linguistic difficulty ..."'. Literary criticism was, he had declared on another occasion, 'a charming parasite'.[33] 'Chatter', 'frivolity', 'mere elegance', 'gossip', 'ornamental', 'an accomplishment', 'charming, but parasitical': the recurrent imagery is too pervasive to be accidental.

There is, then, an inbuilt tension between claims to specialist disciplinary status and to a general civilizing mission, and between the feminization of literature and its claim to 'manly' intellectual rigour. If men of power in industry, as well as their workforce, are to benefit from this civilizing study, it can only be in school in the course of general secondary socialization. Industrial workers are not normally university educated, and industrial managers and 'captains of industry' where they are, do not usually have degrees in English but in subjects more closely tied to their careers, such as industrial and business studies or economics. But if the specific functions and virtues claimed for

English and used to justify its place on the curriculum are achieved for the majority at primary and secondary level or as casual lay readers, then the position of a professional elite making careers out of the study of that subject at university becomes problematic. To become a specialism, English had to establish itself as the preserve of a literary critical elite but to justify its function as a general civilizing and humanizing study it had to be accessible outside that elite.

The second related paradox which had to be negotiated by English studies was its relationship to gender. The institutionalization of literature within the education system created an elite of professionals who were predominantly male. But the majority of its students, and of those who taught English lower down the education system in the schools, were predominantly female.

The ways in which literature and literary studies have negotiated this paradox are many and various. Some are also quite funny. The least successful ploy is that of vehemently affirming its own inherent masculinity. S.M. Gilbert and S. Gubar offer some splendid examples: 'The artist's most essential quality is masterly execution, which is a kind of male gift, and especially marks off men from women ...';[34] 'Jane Austen's novels fail because her writing lacks a strong male thrust',[35] and 'Literary women lack that blood congested genital drive which energises every great style'.[36] They conclude that 'In patriarchal Western culture ... the text's author is a father, an aesthetic patriarch whose pen is an instrument of generative power like his penis'.[37] But actually such ostentatious display of literature's hairy chest merely serves to place its masculine status in doubt. Where masculinity is secure, it need not be strenuously affirmed.

A second common ploy is more sophisticated. It concedes literature's feminine identification, but reserves it nevertheless for men — but men who have a feminine sensibility. John Fowles may serve as an example of this tendency. In that excruciatingly, embarrassingly awful book, *The Aristos*, he informs us that 'there are of course Adam-women and Eve-men; singularly few, among the world's great progressive artists and thinkers, have not belonged to the latter category'.[38]

Finally the contradiction is negotiated in similar terms within literature itself, in its own self-portrait. In an interesting discussion of Joyce's *Portrait of the Artist as a Young Man*, Steve Watts analyses the way that Stephen Daedalus negotiates the gender identities on offer to him in his path to the role of artist. He comments on '... the ability to internalize and *protect* the "feminine" aspects of sensitivity, while at the same time superseding this "feminine" in a new totalizing masculinity of the artist as secular priest of the imagination ... The famous vision of the wading girl exemplifies the way in which what Stephen sees can be transformed into art — into the "image". His sensitivity, his "soul", is figured as feminine, as attested by the personal pronouns that surround it, and it is his soul that cries out in profane joy at the image of the girl — an image which "passes into" that feminine soul. Yet it is *his* soul; he possesses it as he possesses the image: as the artist constructs, forges and possesses (impersonally, not as a man) the female objects which are the matter of his transfiguring art'.[39]

English literature was and still is kept within the custodianship of men, in an elite and specialized humane culture. But at the feet of the male professoriat sit the rank and file of English's missionary undertaking, the mainly female students who will later go out into the schools to transmit its moral message and its civilizing power. The prevailing imagery used not only by the Leavisites but throughout the whole history of the battle for English, from Arnold onwards, is stridently masculine. It evokes not only missionaries, but armies, warriors, crusaders: a veritable secular church militant. Under the influence of the Leavisites '... the mood ... is unmistakeably aggressive — "urgency"; "militancy against all that is hateful" . . . . Teachers, as envisaged by Leavis and Thompson ... must be highly cultivated men of fierce conviction who will inspire their pupils to resist their environment in a similar spirit'.[40] The recurring image is of men addressing boys and urging them, too, on towards a proper manliness. But within the school itself, the image of the teacher is increasingly, as the century progresses, that of the good mother or the kindly nurse. Particularly with the later development of 'progressive' education, the virtues of the ideal teacher become the ability to draw out the child through encouragement, support, warmth, generosity — in a word, to emulate the good mother.[41]

It is clear that women play a major mediating role in cultural and ideological transmission, one which has been largely neglected within Marxist theories of ideology and culture. In female teachers of English, the traditional functions ascribed to both women and literature are combined. Hence the paradox that the cultural heritage within which they are systematically marginalized is nevertheless seen as one which is peculiarly theirs. 'A woman without poetry is like a landscape without sunshine' wrote Sara Ellis in 1842.[42] But the woman poet is another matter altogether.

Women and the Transmission of a Literary Culture

Women act as mediators within the cultural and social formation described by Anderson and Nairn. They mediate a humanist culture and the world of power and property which is the world of men and capital, through their roles as wives, mothers and teachers. Gramsci wrote: '... intellectual activity must also be distinguished in terms of its intrinsic characteristics, according to levels ... at the higher level would be the creators of the various sciences, philosophy, art, etc., and at the lowest the most humble "administrators" and divulgators of pre-existing, traditional, accumulated intellectual wealth'.[43] The mobilization of English in defence of bourgeois hegemony was also a mobilization of women. For it is they who play this more 'humble' role identified by Gramsci, men who reserve to themselves the 'higher' part of cultural production in science and the arts.

Given the way in which the humanities in general and English literature in particular are identified as peculiarly appropriate to, almost the cultural property of, women, the mechanisms whereby this division of labour is achieved by which women are by and large confined to this 'administrative' role are of particular interest. In view of the critical part played by women in the transmission of the literary culture, it is not surprising that the negotiation of gender within that culture presents such a delicate problem. For women must be induced to play this subordinate part if the maintenance of the gender order of domination and subordination is to remain intact. A wholesale feminization of the literary culture would undermine the gender order. This is prevented by excluding women effectively from its upper echelons save as exceptional cases. Clearly this sifting out process occurs during the course of the progression of male and female students of English through the educational system. Women are encouraged to study English and the arts, and channelled into these parts of the curriculum up to the level of higher education, but are cooled out during the course of their university careers and into Gramsci's subordinate administrative roles.

Marxist feminist studies of women and education have on the whole neglected the area of higher education because they have primarily concerned themselves with the fortunes of working-class girls and the manner in which the education system reproduces gender relations along class lines. Working-class girls do not come through to higher education in substantial numbers, and consequently Marxist feminist work on gender and education has focused primarily on earlier stages of the educational process. But this is as shortsighted as the equally prevalent tendency among feminists to study women only. Women, as well as the working class, must know their enemy.

Radical feminism, too, has tended to neglect the study of women in higher education with some notable exceptions such as Adrienne Rich's paper on the 'women-centred university'.[44] Radical feminist analysis of the rights and wrongs of women pays primary attention to the areas of personal relations, marriage and the family because it defines men rather than capitalism as 'the main enemy' and these are the central sites of male-female interpersonal interaction. Radical feminism does not have the Marxist feminist bias against women in higher education because it believes that all women, regardless of their social class, share a common oppression. But it is also less interested than Marxist feminism in either the position of women in the labour market or in the education system because of the central role which has been ascribed to these institutions in the transmission and maintenance of class rather than personal relations. Where radical feminism has looked at the school, it has concentrated its fire on the gender bias of the curriculum and in the very language and practices of instruction. The whole field of study of women and education has in fact been dominated by liberal feminism with its emphasis on 'fairness'. A recent collection of essays on women in higher education was entitled 'Is Higher Education Fair to Women?' (To be fair to its contributors, some of the essays went well beyond the liberal problematic of the title.)[45] The concept of equity goes hand in hand with an emphasis on the individual rather than the collectivity. Its concerns above all are with disparities of opportunity for different types of individual to gain access to the qualifications necessary for the best jobs or to continue to further education.

That the question of fairness is not the most interesting one that can be posed would seem to be a point hardly worth labouring in Marxist feminist circles. Yet the relative neglect of women's place in higher education has left the liberal problematic unchallenged and it recurs in surprising places with all the force of the natural.

One of the few things we do know about women in higher education concerns their academic performance. More men than women are awarded the best and the worst degrees. Women are bunched in the middle of the range. In 1983-4, the 3890 first class degrees awarded by English universities went in a ratio of three to one to men whose representation among the student body as a whole is more like two to one.[16] But overall aggregate figures of this kind disguise important differences within subject areas. The results for English, the subject that concerns us here, reveal a general tendency for women to do relatively less well in those subjects which have a feminine gender identification. In 1979, the last year for which the UGC gave a full breakdown by sex, 3.3 per cent of women gained firsts in English compared to 8.1 per cent of men. Over the period from 1973-9, nearly 9 per cent of men who took degrees in English gained first class honours, compared to an average of less than 4 per cent of women. Thus, shockingly, in the very subject in which girls are given early validation and which is offered to them as peculiarly appropriate — there is widespread consensus from the hapless Tom Tulliver's tutor to contemporary research on gender and educational performance, that girls have a facility with words — they underachieve most markedly at university level. If we look at the progression of girls and women through the levels at which English is taught in our education system it would appear that there must be some powerful cooling out mechanisms in play. For their preponderance at lower levels is thoroughly overturned by the time they arrive at the higher reaches. Table 1 shows a cross section of the numbers of women still present at each stage in the structure from graduation to the professoriate. It clearly reveals this process of attrition. Table 2 reveals it in more graphic form.

A university education in English therefore serves rather different functions for men and women. A relatively high

TABLE 7.1
Men and Women in Departments of England in Universities in England
and Wales, 1979

	Men	Women	Women as % of total
Undergraduates admitted to first year	964	1,929	64.5% (appr.)
Graduates obtaining first class degrees	89	57	39% (appr.)
Postgraduates	475	289	38% (appr.)
Academic staff:			
a. Lecturers	2,719	740	22% (appr.)
b. Readers/Senior Lecturers	966	127	11.5% (appr.)
c. Professors*	672	31	4% (appr.)

*Aggregated figures for Language, Literature, Area Studies & Arts

Source: DES University Statistics 1983-4, vol. 1, Students and Staff,
Cheltenham 1979.

TABLE 7.2
Percentages of Women at Each Level of the Academic Hierarchy

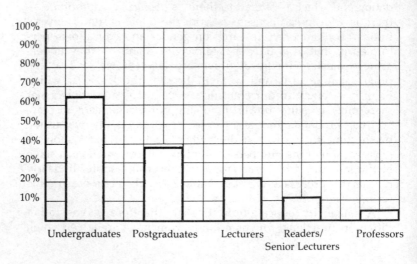

proportion of men get very good degrees and go on to embark on an academic career. A much smaller percentage of women start out on this same path, though in absolute terms the numbers are about equal because more women choose to study English in the first place. But the rate of attrition is much higher among women subsequently and only a minute proportion reach professorial level. The women who study English at university by and large do two things subsequently. They marry professional men and mother their children who are the pool which provides a goodly proportion of the next generation of students and high culture producers and bearers; and they become teachers and, as such, secondary socializers of the next generation. In both roles they are now, as they were in the nineteenth century when they first entered higher education, key agents in the transmission of cultural capital of which they are still unable to take full possession in their own right.

8.
Conclusion

The Cultural Logic of Capitalism

'Where the desires and sensibilities of people in every class have become open-ended and insatiable, attuned to permanent upheavals in every sphere of life, what can possibly keep them fixed and frozen in their bourgeois roles'?[1] Marshall Berman's sketch of capitalism as a dynamic, restless social form which thrives on catastrophe and renewal, disintegration and mobilization, has been criticized for its lack of a sense of history.[2] It could be added that bourgeois roles have always been less fixed and frozen than they might appear to be in that class's preferred self-image. But Berman's is a view of capitalism which decisively forestalls any attempt to found a Marxist theory of culture upon a functionalist logic. Where the ideological 'needs' of capitalism are plural and contradictory, cultural production necessarily pulls in more ways than one: it is simultaneously 'functional' and 'dysfunctional' in relation to capitalism and to its ruling class.

This book began by considering some of the implications of the fact that the novel came to prominence in England in the eighteenth century as a commodity form produced by and for the bourgeoisie. Left cultural theory, in the main, has examined the history of the English novel from the point of view of its articulation with bourgeois ideology. But the ideological bearings and effects of any given component of the national culture are shaped and mediated by the form in which it is produced and distributed. Capitalist cultural production, in producing commodities, is obliged like other departments of capitalist commodity production to consider the profitability of its product as well as the uses and gratifications which it promises to its readers and which serve to generate an effective demand.

The major ideological institutions of capitalist society, those of family, school and church, are supported by sanctions which guarantee the exposure of individuals to their socializing processes. Commodity-culture has no such binding sanctions outside its own capacity to please those who are in a position to consume. While the wants which 'commodities of the fancy' stimulate and address are developed in the course of the emergence of the socialized individual human being, and are therefore not independent of the society and culture within which that socialization occurs, it does not follow that they can be addessed with impunity nor that individual and collective attempts to satisfy them are necessarily '. . . conducive to good order'.[3] Capitalism generates desires and makes implicit promises some of which cannot be made good for anybody and most of which cannot be met for all people and classes under capitalism. But the hopes and also the fears which such desires inspire finds expression above all in capitalist commodity culture.[4] Some of its expressions have the ideological effect of reconciling individuals and classes to gratification indefinitely or even permanently deferred. But the business of capitalist commodity culture is above all to work upon such desires in order to maximize the production of surplus-value. While the result may be good business, whether or not it is 'good literature' or effective ideology cannot be settled a priori. Cultural production of all kinds is leaky with respect to ideological functions and commodity cultural production perhaps especially so.

The principal 'wants of the fancy' which are addressed in commodity culture do not have the same direct relationship to the promises of capitalism as those discussed by Richard Dyer which so pervasively inform mass entertainment's utopian fantasies.[5] They stem from the repressed desires of the unconscious and they provide a most potent means to engage the interest of consumers and to keep them coming back for more. Commodity culture, in addressing, stimulating and negotiating these desires, is again not necessarily conducive to good order.

To call a given component of the national culture an effect of the capitalist transformation of culture into commodities, or to label it bourgeois in the sense that it is produced by and for the bourgeoisie, is therefore to say little of substance. However it *is* to say something: to place some limits on our expectations about what we may find. In moving away from Watt's sociological essentialism which led him to suggest that what we might expect to discover was exclusively an aesthetic of realism, it is not being suggested that the relationship between capitalism and commodity literature is a completely open one, and that the forms which such a literature may take know no bounds. On the contrary, it is absolutely necessary for Marxist cultural analysis to construct some characterization of the national culture in terms of its dominant features and to trace the ways in which these change over time, so that these developments may be related to their social conditions of existence and to changes in capitalism itself.[6]

In his discussion of postmodernism, Jameson suggests that it must be grasped '... not as a style, but rather as a "cultural dominant": a conception which allows for the presence and co-existence of a range of very different but subordinate features'.[7] Postmodernism provides, he argues, a kind of cultural 'field force' which positions all forms of cultural production at the present time. Neither modernism nor postmodernism is touched on in this book since the story which it dips into is suspended more or less at the point in time at which modernism emerged to cultural dominance at the end of the nineteenth century. The discussion in chapter seven of the institutionalization of English takes the story a little further than this it is true. But while the relationship of modernism to academe might prove an interesting topic in its own right, it is not one which is discussed here.

Jameson's idea of a cultural dominant is an interesting one. But cultural dominance may have been differently orchestrated at different times and in different national cultures. Realism can only be seen as the dominant style in the nineteenth-century novel if we restrict ourselves to the consideration of 'high culture': to that species of 'cultural capital' which gained currency as 'literature'. Within this legitimate currency there circulated without a doubt the ideas, values and structures of feeling of the ruling bourgeoisie: but not *all* of the ideas, values and structures of feeling of that class nor *only* in realist literature.

The ideas and values which were foregrounded in literary realism were, it has been suggested, those which that class openly acknowledged and which have been associated with the classic bourgeois virtues so graphically described by Max Weber and associated by him and others with capitalist production. But those wants of the fancy which could not be legitimated or acknowledged within this frame circulated nonetheless and may be considered every bit as much the products of capitalism and the cultural property of the class.

The public and virtuous face of bourgeois rationality was foregrounded through the realist goal of truth-telling, narrative outcomes, and the controlling voice of god-the-narrator which was heard so insistently in much of this type of fiction. It was a voice which spoke in the tones and sentiments of bourgeois virtue and whose comment on the events of the narrative and on the characters who lived them posed the moral question of the time: 'who am I, what shall I do, how shall I live'? Ulterior bourgeois *fancies* might meantime circulate in the narrative itself and the action it described, entertaining other possible outcomes before arriving at its preordained resolution. As George Eliot, the supreme executioner of this type of fictional narration was well aware, the novel's plot creates an emotional economy which moves and engrosses the reader far more effectively than the moral voice of god-the-narrator. And this economy was frequently at variance with the public face of bourgeois ideology and the comment of god-the-narrator.

Through these aesthetic devices of realism and through its self-presentation as literature; and finally through the manner of its institutionalization as a system of production and consumption as described in chapter four, the literary novel in the nineteenth century negotiated its own relationship to the anarchic fancies of the capitalist market-place without the necessity of having to acknowledge that relationship and without unduly disturbing the mask of its more pious face. Bourgeois culture was able to display the bourgeois virtues as though the excesses on which capitalism necessarily draws to market its commodities had nothing to do with capitalism or with the bourgeoisie.

In an era of a more aggressive consumer capitalism it is more difficult, though not impossible, to maintain this mask particularly among the older capitalisms of Europe where such attitudes still survive. Capitalism's traditional intellectuals are still able to maintain their characteristic moral distance from the economic system, including even those intellectuals who staff the capitalist state. The illustrious names cited by Anderson are drawn still from families whose sons are educated at a few public schools and at Oxbridge. Margaret Thatcher and Norman Tebbitt[8] might well agree with Tom Nairn[9] that this cultural formation has out-lived its usefulness and regret the prevalence of anachronistic attitudes towards profit-making and the entrepreneurial spirit cultivated in schools and universities. But they will need to begin the task of rooting it out in the capitalist state itself, in the higher reaches of the civil service which is still overwhelmingly dominated by men schooled in these traditions, trained, many of them, in that very institute of learning which snubbed Thatcher by refusing to grant her an honorary degree.

One reason for the perpetuation of this fiction of distance is the phenomenon of United States cultural imperialism. While this imperialism is real enough, it also provides a convenient scapegoat for European capitalisms' traditional intellectuals. The capitalist culture-industry which the state and the bourgeoisie have been unwilling to own and acknowledge may to some extent be passed off as an alien American import. The critique of mass culture, whether mounted from left or right, has usually been a critique of Americanization,[10] and the contradiction inherent in any capitalist culture may be experienced as a con-tingent difference between national cultures. American culture has always been more brash and more honest, too, in acknow-ledging and celebrating capitalism and its relationship to the market. It has in consequence a certain dynamic quality so often lacking where traditional intellectuals have remained dominant. It is significant that Anderson identifies the impact of mass con-sumption industries based on new technologies as one of his three coordinates of the cultural flowering of the early decades of twentieth-century Europe associated with modernism.[11] For that technology was first developed in the United States as he points out and its spread has been experienced as 'Americanization'.

To repeat, cultural dominance may have been different at dif-ferent moments in time. This book suggests that the dominance of an aesthetic of realism was achieved in part through cultural segregation in the second period of the novel's expansion in the nineteenth century. Realism was dominant in 'high bourgeois' culture; but it coexisted not only with the culture of the masses but also with markedly different bourgeois forms. And realism has not always been the dominant form of bourgeois fiction. In the first period of the novel's expansion, discussed in chapter three, when it was denied the status of literature, the novel was dominated by non-realist fantasy forms such as gothic and the novel of sentiment.

What the constitution of the novel as literature permitted was the filtering out of these non-realist forms from the stock of 'cultural capital'. A word about marginality is in order here. Gothic fiction was marginalized only when looked at from the vantage point of the subsequent construction of 'the great tradition' of literature. As a commodity form of fiction, it was immensely successful. Taking a longer view, it might be argued that with the development of capitalism it was the literary culture itself that was marginalized, commodity forms which were brought to the centre. This long-term process of centering popular, non-realist forms may have merely been subject to a lengthy interruption in the nineteenth century. For Jameson suggests that in the epoch of postmodernism, the boundaries between high and mass culture have become permeable in a way that they were not in the nineteenth century. '... one fundamental feature of all ... postmodernisms ... namely, the effacement in them of the older (essentially high-modernist) frontier between high culture and so-called mass or commercial culture, and the emergence of new kinds of texts infused with the forms, categories and contents of that very Culture Industry so passionately denounced by all the ideologues of the modern, from Leavis and the American New Criticism all the way to Adorno and the Frankfurt School. The postmodernisms have in fact been fascinated by this whole "degraded" language of Schlock and Kitsch of TV series and Readers' Digest culture, of advertising and motels, of the late show and the grade-B Hollywood film, of so-called paraliterature with its airport paperback categories of the gothic and the romance, the popular biography, the murder mystery and science-fiction or fantasy novel: materials they no longer simply "quote", as a Joyce or a Mahler might have done, but incorporate into their very substance'.[12]

This suggestion of Jameson's is taken up with some hesitation, for three reasons. Firstly, although postmodernist high culture has been permeable to mass culture the flow has not been equally great in both directions. The postmodernist avant-garde has not produced a high culture which is popular and accessible, even though its influence can be traced in mainstream commodity culture which is both of these things. Secondly, this notion of an a-moral, uni-dimensional postmodern culture which eschews the old traditional bourgeois virtues as well as its attendant psychoses is difficult to reconcile with other equally pervasive images of late twentieth-century hegemony: those associated with Reagan, Thatcher, and the new right reaffirmation of Victorian values. Thirdly it leads Jameson to attempt the impossible in his own labour of theory-building. He argues that contemporary theory, too, is postmodernist and that this 'field force' is one in which *all* forms of cultural production must make their way. He therefore tries to make his own way within it. Yet he recognizes that postmodernism effaces history, transforming it into a stockhouse of heterogeneous styles which postmodernism raids eclectically and at random. But Jameson's explanation of modernism and postmodernism is rooted in a Marxism which cannot thus efface history: Mandel's theory of late capitalism.[13] We have today many Marxisms including some that might conceivably be described as postmodernist. But *Capital* belongs to a very different cultural epoch and Mandel's Marxism is decidedly not a postmodernist variant. Any Marxism worthy of the name requires recourse to a history posited as 'real'. As has been argued elsewhere, Marxism is a realism.[14]

The Novel as 'Cultural Capital' and the Filter of Literature

The literary critical establishment in the nineteenth century used its criteria of literary value to filter out those currencies in the novel which on these standards were declared counterfeit. On what basis were those criteria erected? This question has not been systematically addressed here. But in chapter six there is a suggestion as to why it is that so few women novelists have passed through the filter. This question raises itself (or ought to) the more forcibly because of the systematic gender-ambiguity of literary production and a literary culture. One task of this book has been to reinsert the question of gender into new left cultural analysis where it has been singularly absent on the whole. It has throughout been emphasized that at every point in the history of the English novel women have played a distinct and crucial role in its production, consumption and transmission. Chapter seven examined the part played by the novel and by women in the transmission of that culture as both were simultaneously admitted to the reaches of higher education. The book has examined the paradox of the filtering out of all but a small number of women's texts from the corpus of cultural capital and the cooling out of women from all but Gramsci's 'humble administrative' roles in the creation and custodianship of that culture, against the backdrop of the distinctively feminine connotations of literature and writing.[15]

However this work argues that the filtering out of women's texts is not usefully understood as a male conspiracy even though it serves to keep women in their proper place in patriarchal capitalism. An attempt has been made to identify the principles under which some women's texts passed through that filter while many more failed to do so in spite of having been immensely successful in their own time. It has been tentatively suggested that it is not so much the sex of the author which secures the exclusion of a text in the process of cultural capitalist accummulation as the address of the text. It is woman-to-woman writing which is excluded. Because those forms have been and continue to be extremely popular they have been drawn upon in the postmodernist high cultural raid upon popular culture, along with forms whose address is not woman-to-woman but whose real as opposed to implied author is often female, such as detective fiction. Clearly there are some circumstances under which women's texts do become cultural capital.

Of those nineteenth-century women whose texts passed through the filter, it has been suggested here that some spoke as women from positions offered to women within the dominant domestic ideology but broke with previous traditions by addressing men as well as women and succeeded in capturing the attention of male readers and critics. Elizabeth Gaskell has been the principal example. But perhaps more frequently, those female authors spoke not specifically as women but as 'human beings' addressing other human beings. Such women often disguised their sex by adopting masculine pseudonyms. George Eliot is the prime example.

However an acceptable form of address in itself clearly was insufficient to guarantee literary success. Chapter seven suggests some additional reasons why the conditions of literary pro-

duction and the rules which coded 'literature' might have oper-
ated against women and in favour of men over and above mere
male prejudice which no doubt added its toll to the long list of
casualties. These are no more than tentative suggestions and
more detailed investigation would be needed to firm them up
into more confident propositions. However it is interesting to
note that there is no parallel unbreachable barrier against the
entry of man-to-man fiction into the corpus of literature. While
man-to-man genres such as the western are excluded, man-to-
man address in 'great literature' such as that exemplified by
Hemingway is by no means uncommon.

Women and the Accumulation of Counter-Cultural Capital

The series in which this book has appeared is called 'Questions
for Feminism'. I argued in my introduction that these questions
are also and crucially questions for Marxism. This book has been
above all else concerned to confront Marxist literary theory with
its own filtering out of women and gender. Yet a feminist series
is traditionally a space in which feminists address each
other. Not that the address of Marxist-feminist theory is
woman-to-woman. Because it is a *Marxist* feminism it cannot be
so restricted and indeed this has been held against it in radical
feminist circles. The charge that the union of Marxism and
feminism has been an unhappy one in which Marxism has
been the dominant, masculine partner is one which tends to
stick.[16] For while Marxist-feminism necessarily addresses
Marxism and men, Marxism by no means necessarily returns
the compliment and listens or engages in dialogue. I have
been struck in doing the reading for this work, by the extent to
which feminist, and Marxist, literary theory talk past each
other. They often simply don't cite each other. This is
particularly noticeable where the texts under examination have
attracted attention from both as is the case with Mary Shelley's
Frankenstein.

Particularly depressing, too, is the almost total exclusion of
questions of gender from the current debate on the left about
modernism and postmodernism.[17] If the things which feminists,
Marxist and non-Marxist, have been saying in the twenty years
or so of the current women's movement have had so little

impact, what hope is there of effecting any permanent shift in left cultural thought which will ensure that women and gender are always central to the frame?

Today, as in the eighteen-nineties, feminism is big business. Every major publishing house now has its 'women's studies' or feminist list. It would perhaps be sobering were we able to look ahead over the next hundred years to see how many of the texts generated by the current explosion of the women's movement will survive any future relegation of 'the woman question' to its traditional place as a secondary question for socialism. How many feminist texts will suffer the fate of woman-to-woman forms to be recovered only with the advent of a new phase of feminism? Marxist counter-culture is in danger of reproducing the gender division of labour which has been characteristic of the dominant culture throughout most of the history of capitalism. If it does so, or substitutes one of its own, then the loss will be one suffered by Marxism as well as by women and feminists.

Notes

Chapter 1

1. Perry Anderson, 'Components of the National Culture', in Alexander Cockburn and Robin Blackburn, eds, *Student Power*, Harmondsworth 1969.
2. Perry Anderson, 'Origins of the Present Crisis', in Perry Anderson and Robin Blackburn, eds, *Towards Socialism*, London 1966.
3. Tom Nairn, *The Break-Up of Britain*, London 1977.
4. Anderson, 'Components . . .', p. 228.
5. Ibid., p. 268.
6. Tom Nairn, 'The English Literary Intelligentsia', *Bananas*, 3, 1976, p. 59.
7. Ibid., p. 63.
8. Ibid., p. 65.
9. Ibid., p. 67.
10. Ibid., p. 76.
11. For a discussion of French and American feminist literary theories, see Toril Moi, *Sexual/Textual Politics: Feminist Literary Theory*, London and New York 1985.
12. Dorothy Smith, 'Women, Class and Family', *The Socialist Register*, London 1983.
13. Ian Watt, *The Rise of the Novel*, London 1957.
14. Ibid., p. 33.
15. Tony Bennett, *Formalism and Marxism*, London 1979, contains a discussion of these developments in Marxist literary theory; also Catherine Belsey, *Critical Practice*, London 1980. Some examples include Terry Eagleton, *Criticism and Ideology*, London 1976; Stuart Hall, 'Culture, the Media and the "Ideological Effect"', in J. Curran, M. Gurevitch and J. Woollacott, eds, *Mass Communication and Society*, London 1977;

Frederick Jameson, *The Political Unconscious*, London 1978; Colin MacCabe, *James Joyce and the Revolution of the Word*, London 1978; Pierre Macheray, *A Theory of Literary Production*, London 1978.

16. Colin MacCabe, 'Realism and the Cinema', *Screen*, vol 15, no 2, 1974.

17. Dale Spender, *Mothers of the Novel*, London 1986.

18. Raymond Williams, *Keywords*, London 1976, p. 218.

19. John Tinnon Taylor, *Early Opposition to the English Novel*, New York 1943, p. v.

20. Ibid., p. 84.

21. Ibid., p. 80.

22. Ibid., p. 83.

23. Ibid., p. 83.

24. Ibid., p. 110.

25. Ibid., p. 59.

26. David Punter, *The Literature of Terror*, London 1980.

27. Karl Marx, *Capital*, vol. 1, London 1970, p. 35.

28. For a recent study of fiction from the point of view of consumption in the late Victorian period, see Rachel Bowlby, *Just Looking: Consumer Culture in Dreiser, Gissing and Zola*, New York and London 1985.

29. Louis James, *Fiction for the Working Man, 1830-1850*, Oxford 1963, and Margaret Dalzeil, *Popular Fiction 100 Years Ago*, London 1957.

30. John Sutherland, *Victorian Novels and their Publishers*, London 1976.

31. Ibid., p. 44.

32. Mario Praz, *The Romantic Agony*, Cambridge 1970.

33. Margaret Mathieson, *The Preachers of Culture*, London 1975.

34. See Josephine Kamm, *Hope Deferred: Girls' Education in English History*, London 1965; Margaret J. Tuke, *A History of Bedford College for Women, 1849-1937*, London 1939; Elaine Kaye, *A History of Queen's College, London*, London 1972, and Brian Doyle, 'The Hidden History of English Studies', in Peter Widdowson, ed., *Re-Reading English*, London and New York 1982.

35. Antonio Gramsci, *Selections From the Prison Notebooks*, London 1971, p. 13.

36. Pierre Bourdieu and Jean Claude Passeron, *Reproduction in Education, Society and Culture*, London 1977.

37. Max Weber, *The Protestant Ethic and the Spirit of Capitalism*, London 1930.

38. G. Lukacs, *Writer and Critic*, London 1970. See especially the essays entitled 'Narrate or Describe', and 'Art and Objective Truth'.

39. Terry Lovell, *Pictures of Reality*, London 1980.

40. Louis Althusser, *Lenin and Philosophy*, London 1971.

41. Raymond Williams, 'Literature and Sociology: in Memory of

Lucien Goldmann', *New Left Review*, 67, 1971.
42. Terry Eagleton, *Literary Theory*, Oxford 1983.
43. Janet Wolff, *Aesthetics and the Sociology of Art*, London 1983.
44. Louis Althusser, *Lenin and Philosophy*, especially chapter on 'Ideology and Ideological State Apparatuses'. See also the references under note 15.
45. Marshall Berman, *All That is Solid Melts into Air*, London 1983.
46. Rosalind Williams, *Dream Worlds; Mass Consumption in Late Nineteenth-Century France*, Berkeley, Los Angeles and London 1982.
47. Bowlby, *Just Looking*.

Chapter 2

1. Terry Eagleton, *Criticism and Ideology*, London 1976; *Literary Theory*, Oxford 1983; *The Functions of Criticism*, London 1984; *The Rape of Clarissa*, Oxford 1982.
2. Dale Spender, *Mothers of the Novel*.
3. Watt, pp. 12-13.
4. Ibid., p. 16.
5. Ibid., p. 27.
6. Weber, *Protestant Ethic*.
7. Watt, p. 61.
8. Ibid., p. 264.
9. MacCabe, 'Realism and the Cinema'.
10. Watt, p. 21.
11. Ibid., p. 298.
12. Eagleton, *Criticism and Ideology*.
13. Gramsci, p. 18.
14. Richard Johnson, 'Barrington Moore, Perry Anderson and English Social Development', in Stuart Hall et al, eds, *Culture, Media, Language: Working Papers in Cultural Studies, 1972-79*, London 1980, p. 66.
15. Malcolm Easton, *Artists and Writers in Paris: the Bohemian Idea, 1803-1867*, London 1964.
16. Howard Becker, *Art Worlds*, Berkeley, Los Angeles and London 1982.
17. Cesar Grāna, *Modernity and its Discontents*, New York, Evanston and London 1964.
18. Jane Austen, *Northanger Abbey*, Penguin Edition, Harmondsworth 1972, pp. 57-8.
19. Kathleen Tillotson, *Novels of the Eighteen-Forties*, Oxford 1954.
20. For example, see Arnold Kettle, *An Introduction to the English Novel*, vol 1, London 1951; Tom Nairn, 'The English Literary Intelligentsia'; and Raymond Williams, *Culture and Society*, London 1960.

21. Praz, *The Romantic Agony*.
22. Quoted in Grāna, p. xv.
23. Praz, p. 348.
24. William Gaunt, *The Aesthetic Adventure*, London 1945.
25. Karl Marx, *Grundrisse*, London 1973, p. 287.
26. Simon Frith, *Sound Effects: Youth, Leisure, and the Politics of Rock and Roll*, New York 1981.
27. Ibid., p. 254.
28. Peter Bailey, *Leisure and Class in Victorian England*, Toronto 1978.
29. Gaunt, p. 40.
30. Rosalind Williams, p. 69.
31. Ibid.
32. W.R. Greg, 'Why are Women Redundant?', *National Review*, April 1862, quoted in Patricia Hollis, ed., *Women in Public: the Women's Movement 1850-1900*, London 1979, p. 38.
33. Eagleton, *The Functions of Criticism*.
34. Catherine Hall, 'Gender Divisions and Class Formation in the Birmingham Middle Class; 1780-1850', in R. Samuel, ed., *People's History and Socialist Theory*, London 1981.
35. Eli Zaretsky, *Capitalism, the Family and Personal Life*, London 1976.
36. Erving Goffman, *The Presentation of Self in Everyday Life*, London 1969.
37. Leonore Davidoff, 'Class and Gender in Victorian England', in Judith L. Newton, Mary P. Ryan and Judith R. Walkowitz, eds, *Sex and Class in Women's History*, London 1983.
38. Lawrence Stone, *The Family, Sex and Marriage in England, 1500-1800*, London, 1977.
39. Ellen Malos, ed., *The Politics of Housework*, London 1980.
40. Patricia Branca, *Silent Sisterhood*, London 1975.
41. John Sutherland, *Fiction and the Fiction Industry*, London 1978, p. 19.
42. Watt, p. 310.
43. Elaine Showalter, *A Literature of Their Own*, London 1979, p. 37.
44. Ibid., p. 53.
45. Ibid., p. 53.
46. Ibid., p. 55.
47. Claire Tomalin, *The Life and Death of Mary Wollstonecraft*, London 1974.
48. Spender, *Mothers of the Novel*.
49. R.D. Altick, *The English Common Reader*, Chicago 1957.
50. Mary Poovey, *The Proper Lady and the Woman Writer*, Chicago 1984.
51. Jane Spencer, *The Rise of the Woman Novelist*, Oxford 1986. This interesting and scholarly study of the woman writer in the eighteenth century appeared when this work was already completed.

Chapter 3

1. David Punter, *The Literature of Terror*, London 1980.
2. Altick, p. 50.
3. Ibid., p. 62.
4. James.
5. Dalziel.
6. Guinivere L. Griest, *Mudie's Circulating Library and the Victorian Novel*, Newton Abbot 1970, p. 51.
7. Taylor, ch. II. See also Altick and Griest.
8. Altick, p. 62.
9. Dorothy Blakey, *The Minerva Press*, Oxford 1939, p. 29 f.
10. Taylor.
11. Altick, p. 58.
12. Blakey, p. 6.
13. Ibid., p. 54.
14. Ibid., p. 57.
15. J.M.S. Tompkins, *The Popular Novel in England, 1770-1800*, London 1932.
16. Ibid., p. 120.
17. For example see Ien Ang, *Watching Dallas*, London and New York 1985; Charlotte Brunsdon, 'Crossroads: Notes on a Soap Opera', *Screen*, vol. 22, no. 4, 1981; Richard Dyer et al, *Coronation Street*, London 1981; Dorothy Hobson, *Crossroads: the Drama of a Soap Opera*, London 1982, and Tania Modleski, *Loving with a Vengeance*, New York and London 1982.
18. Tompkins, p. 19.
19. Punter, p. 27.
20. Ibid., p. 425.
21. Marilyn Butler, *Romantics, Rebels and Reactionaries: English Literature and its Background, 1760-1830*, Oxford 1981.
22. Ibid., p. 23.
23. Ibid., p. 55.
24. Ibid., p. 36.
25. Ibid., p. 23.
26. Ibid., p. 31.
27. Tzvetan Todorov, *The Fantastic*, Cornell 1973.
28. Ibid., p. 25.
29. Mary Shelley, *Frankenstein*, Penguin Edition, Peter Fairclough, ed., *Three Gothic Novels*, Harmondsworth 1968, p. 449.
30. Ibid., p. 477.
31. Todorov, p. 158.
32. Ibid., p. 168.
33. Rosemary Jackson, *Fantasy: the Literature of Subversion*, London and New York 1981.

34. Ibid., p. 173.
35. Ibid., p. 174.
36. Ibid., p. 140.
37. Ibid., p. 176.
38. Ibid., p. 179.
39. Ibid., p. 103.
40. Ibid., p. 121.
41. Poovey.
42. Jackson, p. 103.
43. Ellen Moers, *Literary Women*, London 1978.
44. Shelley, p. 264.
45. Marilyn Butler, in a talk delivered at Warwick University in 1986 which was based on a forthcoming book.
46. Poovey, p. 126.
47. Ibid., p. 133.
48. Franco Moretti, *Signs Taken for Wonders*, London 1983.
49. Ibid., p. 85.
50. Butler, Warwick University talk.
51. Todorov, p. 33.
52. Moretti, p. 105.
53. Ibid., p. 38.
54. Ibid., pp. 38-9.
55. S. Freud and J. Breuer, *Studies in Hysteria*, Pelican Freud Library, vol. 13, 1974, p. 393.
56. Catherine Hall, 'Gender Divisions . . .'.

Chapter 4

1. Tillotson, *Novels of the Eighteen-Forties*.
2. Robert Escarpit, *Sociology of Literature*, London 1971.
3. Dates are inevitably a little arbitrary. 1894 is identified as the cut-off point because of the demise of the three-decker novel in that year. See Griest, p. 171.
4. John Sutherland, *Victorian Novels*, p. 4.
5. Arthur Waugh, *A Hundred Years of Publishing*, London 1930, p. 4.
6. Sutherland, *Victorian Novels*.
7. Griest, p. 18.
8. Ibid., p. 21.
9. Sutherland, *Victorian Novels*, p. 5.
10. Williams, *Dream Worlds*.
11. Walter Benjamin, 'The Work of Art in the Age of Mechanical Reproduction', in Benjamin, *Illuminations*, London 1970.
12. Becker, *Art Worlds*.

13. Ruby V. Redinger, *George Eliot: the Emergent Self*, London, Sydney and Toronto 1975, p. 384.

14. Ibid., p. 449.

15. Ibid., p. 414.

16. George Eliot, 'Leaves from a Notebook', in Thomas Pinney, ed., *Essays of George Eliot*, London 1963, p. 448.

17. Patrick Brantlinger, Ian Adams and Sheldon Rothblatt, 'The French Lieutenant's Woman: a Discussion', *Victorian Studies*, XV, 1971-2, and Ronald Binns, 'John Fowles: Radical Romancer,' *Critical Quarterley*, XV, 1973.

18. Sutherland, *Victorian Novels*, p. 211.

19. R.D. Altick, 'The Sociology of Authorship', *Bulletin of New York Public Library*, LXVI, 1962, p. 392.

20. Watt, p. 202.

21. Showalter, p. 37.

22. Margherita Rendel, 'Women Academics in the Seventies', in Sandra Acker and David Warren Piper, eds, *Is Higher Education Fair to Women?*, Guildford 1984.

23. Dale Spender, *Mothers of the Novel*.

24. Dale Spender, *Man-Made Language*, London 1980, p. 147.

25. For example see Nina Auerbach, *Communities of Women*, Cambridge, Mass. 1978; Sandra M. Gilbert and Susan Gubar, *The Madwoman in the Attic; the Woman Writer and the Nineteenth Century Literary Imagination*, New Haven 1979; Mary Jacobus, ed., *Women Writing and Writing about Women*, London 1979; Juliet Mitchell, *Women: the Longest Revolution. Essays in Feminism, Literature and Psychoanalysis*, London 1984; Ellen Moers, *Literary Women*, London 1978; Patricia Meyer Spaacks, *The Female Imagination*, London 1976; Elaine Showalter, *A Literature of Their Own*, London 1979.

26. Since I wrote this a new biography of Gaskell has appeared in the Berg Women's Series: Tessa Brodetsky, *Elizabeth Gaskell*, London 1986.

27. Barbara Taylor, *Eve and the New Jerusalem*, London 1983, p. 112.

28. Branca attempted to reconstruct the popular image of the middle-class 'lady' by shifting the focus to her less well-heeled middle-class sisters — those whose family income was between £100-£300 per annum. This income would take them into the realm of 'surplus consumption' but on a modest scale which would require careful budgeting and which ruled out the possibility of employing domestic servants in sufficient numbers to make the household labour of wives and daughters expendable.

Branca's frame of reference is the theory of 'modernization', and she defines class in terms of income and occupation rather than social relations. The literature of 'modernization' defines that process in terms which foreground the male bourgeoisie. Branca rewrites the story, giving it a heroine who effected a comparable revolutionary modernization of home, family, and personal life. While this rounds out the story, it does nothing to resolve the fundamental inadequacies of the theory.

29. Poovey, p. 15.

30. Judy Simons, 'Fanny Burney: Ambivalent Feminist', paper delivered to the Women and Writing Conference, Sheffield 1983 (unpublished). See Judy Simons, *Fanny Burney*, Macmillan, London 1987.

31. Ang, *Watching Dallas*.

32. Williams, *Culture and Society*.

33. Ibid., p. 87.

34. Ibid., p. 89.

35. Elizabeth Haldane, *Mrs Gaskell and her Friends*, London 1930, p. 47.

36. Williams, *Culture and Society*, p. 88.

37. Quoted in Winifred Gerin, *Elizabeth Gaskell: a Biography*, Oxford 1976, p. 230.

38. Elizabeth Gaskell, *Cousin Phillis and Other Tales*, Oxford World Classics Edition, Oxford 1981, p. 289.

39. Elizabeth Gaskell, *Mary Barton*, Penguin Edition, Harmondsworth 1970, p. 254.

40. Quoted in Gerin, p. 72.

41. Gaskell, *Cousin Phillis*, p. 289.

42. Ibid., p. 291.

43. Moretti, p. 105.

44. Gaskell, *Mary Barton*, p. 220.

Chapter 5

1. Branca, *Silent Sisterhood*.

2. Hollis, pp. 31-40.

3. Quoted in Elizabeth Gaskell, *Life of Charlotte Brontë*, London 1919, p. 127.

4. Gerin, p. 261.

5. Grant Allen, 'Plain Words on the Woman Question', *Fortnightly Review*, Oct 1889, quoted in Hollis, p. 30.

6. 'Queen Bee or Worker Bee', *Saturday Review*, 12 Nov 1859, quoted in Hollis, p. 11.

7. Judith R. Walkowitz, 'Science, Feminism and Romance: The Men and Women's Club, 1885-1889', *History Workshop Journal*, 21, Spring 1986.

8. Ray Strachey, *The Cause*, London 1978.

9. Judith R. Walkowitz, *Prostitution and Victorian Society*, Cambridge 1980.

10. Josephine Butler, *An Autobiographical Memoir*, London 1911, pp. 107-8.

11. Anne Summers, 'A Home from Home — Women's Philanthropic Work in the Nineteenth Century', in Sandra Burman, ed., *Fit Work for Women*, London 1979.

12. Lee Holcombe, *Wives and Property: Reform of the Married Women's Property Law in Nineteenth Century England*, London 1983.

13. Millicent Fawcett, 'Female Suffrage: a Reply', *The Nineteenth Century*, July 1889, quoted in Hollis, p. 331.

14. Olive Banks, *Faces of Feminism*, Oxford 1981.

15. Cathy Porter, *Alexandra Kollontai: a Biography*, London 1980.

16. Catherine Hall, 'Gender Divisions . . .'; also Catherine Hall, 'The Early Formation of Victorian Domestic Ideology', in Burman.

17. Patricia Stubbs, *Women and Fiction: Feminism and the Novel*, 1880-1920, London 1979.

18. Gail Cunningham, *The New Woman and the Victorian Novel*, London and Basingstoke 1978.

19. John Goode, 'Woman and the Literary Text', in Juliet Mitchell and Ann Oakley, eds, *The Rights and Wrongs of Women*, Harmondsworth 1976.

20. George Meredith, in a letter, quoted in Jack Lindsay, *George Meredith; his Life and Works*, London 1956, p. 262.

21. See Lorna Sage's introduction to George Meredith, *Diana of the Crossways*, Virago Edition, London 1980.

22. Simons, *Fanny Burney*.

23. Meredith, p. 189.

24. Ibid., p. 149.

25. Ibid., p. 132.

26. Ibid., p. 103.

27. Ibid., p. 22.

28. Ibid., pp. 88-9.

29. Goode, 'Woman and the Literary Text'.

30. Lindsay, p. 137.

31. Deirdre David, 'Ideologies of Patriarchy, Feminism, and Fiction in *The Odd Women*', *Feminist Studies*, vol. 10, Spring 1984.

32. George Gissing, *The Odd Women*, Virago Edition, London 1980.

33. Ibid., p. 189.

34. Lee Holcombe, *Victorian Ladies at Work*, Newton Abbot 1973.

35. Gissing, p. 174.

36. Ibid., p. 170.

37. John Goode, *George Gissing: Ideology and Fiction*, London 1978, p. 114.

38. Gissing, p. 54.

39. Ibid., p. 20.

40. Ibid., p. 261.

172

41. Ibid., p. 148.
42. Ibid., p. 336.

Chapter 6

1. Anonymous, quoted in Jane Horowitz Murray, *Strong-Minded Women*, Harmondsworth 1982, p. 235.
2. Sojourner Truth, quoted in Angela Davis, *Women, Race and Class*, London 1981, p. 61.
3. Davis. Also Bell Hooks, *Ain't I a Woman? Black Women and Feminism*, London 1981.
4. Derek Hudson, *Munby, Man of Two Worlds: the Life and Dairies of Arthur J. Munby, 1828-1910*, London 1972; and Hannah Cullwick, *Diaries of Hannah Cullwick*, edited by Liz Stanley, London 1984.
5. Quoted in Davis, p. 11.
6. Gillian Kersley, *Darling Madame: Sarah Grand and Devoted Friend*, London 1983, p. 14.
7. Ibid., p. 74.
8. Ibid., p. 87.
9. Ann Brontë, *The Tenant of Wildfell Hall*, Penguin Edition, Harmondsworth 1979.
10. Sarah Grand, *The Heavenly Twins*, London 1893, p. 458.
11. Mona Caird, *The Daughters of Danaus*, London 1894; Mary Cholmondeley, *Red Pottage*, Virago Edition, London 1985.
12. Grand, p. 197.
13. Sarah Grand, *The Beath Book*, Virago Edition, London 1980, p. 68.
14. Kersley, *Darling Madame*.
15. Grand, *The Beth Book*, p. 281.
16. John Berger, *Ways of Seeing*, Harmondsworth 1972.
17. Roland Barthes, 'An Introduction to the Structural Analysis of Narrative', *New Literary History*, 6, 1975.
18. Tania Modleski, *Loving With a Vengeance*.
19. Kersley, p. 70.
20. Ibid., p. 69.
21. Ibid., p. 94.
22. Olive Schreiner, *From Man to Man*, Virago Edition, London 1982.
23. George Egerton, *Keynotes and Discords*, Virago Edition, London 1983.
24. The question of who is included, who not, is of course debatable, and judgements shift over time. But I offer this anecdote in support of my contention about Gissing and Meredith: I was asked recently to contribute a monograph on Jane Austen to a radical critical series whose object was to re-analyse the canon from a left perspective. I offered to take on Gissing instead, and received the rather shamefaced response

that Gissing was not to be included in the series. The acid test seems to be whether or not the writer was studied at A-level. Even demystification of the canon must stay strictly within its boundaries.

Chapter 7

1. Chris Baldick, *The Social Mission of English Criticism*, London 1983; Francis Mulhern, *The Moment of Scrutiny*, London 1979; D.J. Palmer, *The Rise of English Studies*, London, New York and Toronto 1965.
2. John Sutherland, *Fiction and the Fiction Industry*, London 1978, p. 150.
3. Baldick, op. cit.
4. Jane Austen and Another Lady, *Sanditon*, London 1975.
5. Waugh, *A Hundred Years of Publishing*.
6. Hutchinson's New Authors Series, launched in 1957, was supported by more commercial ventures and established several new writers, including Beryl Bainbridge. See Sutherland, *Fiction and the Fiction Industry*, p. 9.
7. Bernard Bergonzi, *The Situation of the Novel*, London 1970.
8. Bernard Bergonzi, Introduction to the Penguin Edition of George Gissing's *New Grub Street*, Harmondsworth 1968.
9. Joyce Senders Pedersen, 'Schoolmistresses and Headteachers: Elites and Education in Nineteenth Century England', *Journal of British Studies*, Autumn 1975.
10. Matthew Arnold, *Culture and Anarchy*, Cambridge 1935.
11. Robert Lowe, Speech to the House of Commons, 15 July 1867, *Parliamentary Debates*, CLXXVIII, cols 1548-9.
12. Margaret Mathieson, *The Preachers of Culture*, London 1975.
13. Holcombe, *Victorian Ladies at Work*.
14. Strachey, ch. IX.
15. Sara Delamont, 'The Contradictions in Ladies' Education'; and 'The Domestic Ideology and Women's Education', in S. Delamont and L. Duffin, eds, *The Nineteenth Century Woman, Her Cultural and Physical World*, London 1978.
16. Ibid.
17. Dale Spender, *Man-Made Language*.
18. Virginia Woolf, *A Room of One's Own*, Triad Panther Edition, London 1977.
19. Mulhern, p. 26.
20. Terry Lovell, 'Writing Like a Woman: a Question of Politics', in Francis Barker et al, *The Politics of Theory*, Colchester 1983.
21. Elizabeth Gaskell, *North and South*, Penguin Edition, Harmondsworth 1970.
22. Gaskell, *Mary Barton*, p. 220.

174

23. Ibid., p. 58.
24. Charlotte Brontë, *Shirley*, Penguin Edition, Harmondsworth 1974.
25. Mathieson.
26. David Williams, *Mr George Eliot; a Biography of George Henry Lewes*, London 1983.
27. Michael Faraday, quoted in G.M. Young, *Victorian England*, London 1960, p. 97.
28. Mulhern, p. 6.
29. Mathieson, p. 135.
30. Baldick, p. 73.
31. Ibid., p. 75.
32. Ibid., p. 96.
33. Mulhern, p. 31.
34. Gerard Manley Hopkins, quoted in Gilbert and Gubar, p. 9.
35. Anthony Burgess, quoted in Gilbert and Gubar, p. 9.
36. William Gass, quoted in Gilbert and Gubar, p. 9.
37. Gilbert and Gubar, p. 6.
38. John Fowles, *The Aristos*, Triad Granada Edition, London 1981, p. 157.
39. Steve Watts, 'Masculinity and the Practice of Teaching', in Helen Taylor, ed., *Literature Teaching Politics*, 6, 1985 Conference Papers, Bristol Polytechnic 1985, p. 64. Elaine Showalter has identified a further strategy for dealing with this paradox in the development of various forms of 'scientific' criticism which turn away from the old humanist rationale for the discipline: 'The new sciences of the text based on linguistics, computers, genetic structuralism, deconstructionalism, neoformalism and deformalism, affective stylistics and psychoaesthetics, have offered literary critics the opportunity to demonstrate that the work they do is as manly and aggressive as nuclear physics. . . .' Elaine Showalter, 'Towards a Feminist Poetics', in Jacobus, p. 38.
40. Mathieson, p. 165.
41. Carolyn Steedman, 'Prisonhouses', *Feminist Review*, 20, Summer 1985.
42. Sara Ellis, quoted in Hollis, p. 15.
43. Gramsci, p. 13.
44. Adrienne Rich, 'Towards a Woman-Centred University', in Rich, *On Lies, Secrets, and Silence: Selected Prose, 1966-1978*, London 1980.
45. Acker and Piper, eds.
46. All figures quoted in this section are taken from Department of Education and Science, *University Statistics*, and *Statistical Abstracts of the UK*, HMSO, 1920-55.

Chapter 8

1. Marshall Berman, *All That is Solid Melts into Air*, London 1983, p. 96.

2. Perry Anderson, 'Modernity and Revolution', *New Left Review*, 144, 1984.

3. Frith, p. 253.

4. Richard Dyer, 'Entertainment and Utopia', *Movie*, 24, 1978.

5. Ibid.

6. This point is made by Anderson, in 'Modernity and Revolution'.

7. Fredric Jameson, 'Postmodernism, or the Cultural Logic of Late Capitalism', *New Left Review*, 146, 1984, p. 56.

8. 'Mrs Thatcher, reinforcing Norman Tebbit's attack on social prejudice against money-making, denounced what she said was a tendency to "downgrade wealth-creators". Nowhere is this attitude more marked than in the cloister and the common-room. Some of Britain's finest companies, she said, were started by people who "didn't speak with Oxford accents" and "hadn't got what people call the right connections".' Quoted in *The Sunday Times*, 24 Mar 1985.

9. Nairn, *The Break-Up of Britain*.

10. See for example, the work of the Frankfurt School, in Ernst Bloch, et al, *Aesthetics and Politics*, New York 1979; Herbert Marcuse, *One-Dimensional Man*, London 1964; C.W. Bigsby, ed., *Superculture: American Popular Culture and Europe*, London 1975. For an overview of the mass culture debate, see Alan Swingewood, *The Myth of Mass Culture*, London 1977.

11. Anderson, 'Modernity and Revolution', p. 106.

12. Jameson, 'Postmodernism . . .', p. 55.

13. Ernest Mandel, *Late Capitalism*, London 1975.

14. Lovell, *Pictures of Reality*.

15. Gramsci, p. 13.

16. Lydia Sargeant, ed., *The Unhappy Marriage of Marxism and Feminism*, London 1981.

17. Angela McRobbie, Review of Marshall Berman, *All That is Solid Melts into Air*, London 1983, *Feminist Review*, 18, 1984.

Bibliography

Elizabeth Abel, ed, *Writing and Sexual Difference*, London 1982.
M.H. Abrams, *The Mirror and the Lamp*, New York 1953.
Sandra Acker & David Warren Piper, *Is Higher Education Fair to Women?* London 1984.
Richard Altick, *The English Common Reader: a Social History of the Mass Reading Public, 1800-1900*, Chicago 1957.
——, 'The Sociology of Authorship', *Bulletin of the New York Public Library*, LXVI, 1962.
Perry Anderson, 'The Origins of the Present Crisis', in P. Anderson & R. Blackburn, eds, *Towards Socialism*, London 1966.
——, 'Components of the National Culture', in A. Cockburn & R. Blackburn, eds, *Student Power*, Harmondsworth 1969.
——, 'Modernity and Revolution', *New Left Review*, 144, 1984.
Ien Ang, *Watching Dallas*, London & New York 1985.
Nina Auerbach, *Communities of Women*, Cambridge, Mass. 1978.
Peter Bailey, *Leisure and Class in Victorian England*, Toronto 1978.
Chris Baldick, *The Social Mission of English Criticism*, London 1983.
Olive Banks, *Faces of Feminism*, Oxford 1981.
P. Baran & P. Sweezy, *Monopoly Capitalism*, Harmondsworth 1968.
Michele Barrett, *Women's Oppression Today*, London 1980.
J. Batsleer et al, *Rewriting English: Cultural Politics of Gender and Class*, London and New York 1985.
Howard Becker, *Art Worlds*, Berkeley, Los Angeles & London 1982.
Gillian Beer, *Darwin's Plots*, London 1983.
——, *George Eliot*, London 1985.
Catherine Belsey, *Critical Practice*, London 1980
Walter Benjamin, *Illuminations*, London 1970.
Tony Bennett, *Formalism and Marxism*, London 1979.
John Berger, *Ways of Seeing*, Harmondsworth 1972.
Bernard Bergonzi, *The Situation of the Novel*, London 1970.

Marshall Berman, *All That is Solid Melts into Air*, London 1982.

C.W. Bigsby, ed, *Superculture: American Popular Culture and Europe*, London 1975.

Kathleen Blake, *Love and the Woman Question in Victorian Literature*, London 1985.

Dorothy Blakey, *The Minerva Press*, Oxford 1939.

Ernst Bloch et al, *Aesthetics and Politics*, New York 1979.

Wayne C. Booth, *The Rhetoric of Fiction*. Chicago 1983.

Pierre Bourdieu and Jean-Claude Passeron, *Reproduction in Education, Society and Culture*, London 1977.

Rachel Bowlby, *Just Looking*, London 1985.

Patricia Branca, *Silent Sisterhood*, London 1975.

Tessa Brodetsky, *Elizabeth Gaskell*, London 1986

Charlotte Brunsdon, 'Crossroads: Notes on a Soap Opera', *Screen*, 22, 4, 1981.

Josephine Butler, *An Autobiographical Memoir*, London 1911.

Marilyn Butler, *Jane Austen and the War of Ideas*, Oxford 1975.

——, *Romantics, Rebels and Reactionaries*, Oxford 1981.

Eileen M. Byrne, *Women and Education*, London 1978.

G.M. Carsanagia, R.H, Freeburn, F.W.J. Hemmings, J.M. Ritchie and J.D. Rutherford, *The Age of Realism*, London 1978.

Nancy Chodorow, *The Reproduction of Mothering*, Los Angeles 1978.

John Clarke, *The Devil Makes Work: Leisure in Capitalist Britain*, London 1985.

Claude Cockburn, *Bestsellers*, London 1986.

A.S. Collins, *Authorship in the Days of Johnson*, London 1927.

——, *The Profession of Letters*, London 1928.

Anna Theresa Cosslett, *The 'Scientific Movement' and Victorian Literature*, London 1985.

George E. Creeger, ed, *George Eliot: a Collection of Critical Essays*, New Jersey 1970.

Hannah Cullwick, *Diaries of Hannah Cullwick*, edited by Liz Stanley, London 1984.

Gail Cunningham, *The New Woman and the Victorian Novel*, London 1978.

H. Cunningham, *Leisure and the Industrial Revolution*, London 1980.

Margaret Dalzeil, *Popular Fiction 100 Years Ago*, London 1957.

Deirdre David, 'Ideologies of Patriarchy, Feminism and Fiction in *The Odd Women*', *Feminist Studies*, 10, 1984.

Leonore Davidoff, 'Class and Gender in Victorian England', in J.L. Newton, M.P. Ryan and J.R. Walkowitz, eds, *Sex and Class in Women's History*, London 1983.

Leonore Davidoff and Catherine Hall, *Family Fortunes: Men and Women of the English Middle Class, 1780-1850*, London 1987.

Angela Davis, *Women, Race and Class*, London 1981.

S. Delamont and L. Duffin, eds, *The Nineteenth Century Woman, her Cul-*

tural and Physical World, London 1978.

Christine Delphy, *Close to Home: a Materialist Analysis of Women's Oppression*, London 1984.

M. Dobb, *Studies in the Development of Capitalism*, London 1963.

Brian Doyle, 'The Hidden History of English Studies', in P. Widdowson, ed, *Re-Reading English*, London & New York 1982.

Alistair M. Duckworth, *The Improvement of the Estate: a Study of Jane Austen's Works*, Baltimore 1971.

Richard Dyer et al., *Coronation Street*, London 1981.

——, 'Entertainment and Utopia', *Movie*, 24, 1978.

Mary Eagleton, ed, *Feminist Literary Theory: a Reader*, Oxford 1986.

Terry Eagleton, *Criticism and Ideology*, London 1976.

——, *The Rape of Clarissa*, Oxford 1982.

——, *Literary Theory*, Oxford 1983.

——, *The Functions of Criticism*, London 1984.

M. Easton, *Artists and Writers in Paris*, London 1964.

Zillah R. Eisenstein, ed, *Capitalist Patriarchy and the Case for Socialist Feminism*, London & New York 1979.

George Eliot, *Essays*, edited by Thomas Pinney, London 1968.

——, *Letters*, edited by Gordon S. Haight, 7 vols, London 1954-5.

E.M. Elliott, 'The Political Economy of English Dissent', in R.M. Hartwell, ed, *The Industrial Revolution*, Oxford 1970.

Robert Escarpit, *Sociology of Literature*, London 1971.

Julien E. Fleenor, ed, *The Female Gothic*, London 1983.

Simon Frith, *Sound Effects: Youth, Leisure and the Politics of Rock and Roll*, New York 1981.

Northrop Frye, *A Study of English Romanticism*, London 1968.

——, *The Secular Scripture*, Cambridge, Mass. 1976.

William Gaunt, *The Aesthetic Adventure*, London 1975.

Per Gedin, *Fiction in the Market Place*, London 1977.

Margaret George, 'From "Goodwife" to "Mistress": the Transformation of the Female in Bourgeois Culture', *Science and Society*, 37, 1973.

Winifred Gerin, *Elizabeth Gaskell: a Biography*, Oxford 1976.

Sandra M. Gilbert and Susan Gubar, *The Madwoman in the Attic*, New Haven 1979.

Erving Goffman, *The Presentation of Self in Everyday Life*, London 1969.

John Goode, 'Woman and the Literary Text', in J. Mitchell and A. Oakley, eds, *The Rights and Wrongs of Women*, Harmondsworth 1976.

——, *George Gissing: Ideology and Fiction*, London 1978.

Nelson Goodman, *The Languages of Art*, London 1969.

Antonio Gramsci, *Selections from the Prison Notebooks*, London 1971.

C. Graña, *Modernity and its Discontents*, New York, Evanston and London 1964.

Guinivere L. Griest, *Mudie's Circulating Library and the Victorian Novel*, Newton Abbot 1970.

Gordon S. Haight, *George Eliot: a Biography*, Oxford 1968.

Elizabeth Haldane, *Mrs Gaskell and her Friends*, London 1930.

Catherine Hall, 'The Early Formation of Victorian Domestic Ideology', in S. Burman ed, *Fit Work for Women*, London 1979.

——, 'Gender Division and Class Formation in the Birmingham Middle Class; 1780-1850', in R. Samuel, ed, *People's History and Socialist Theory*, London 1981.

Stuart Hall, 'Culture, the Media and the "Ideological Effect"', in J. Curran, M. Gurevitch & J. Woollacott, eds, *Mass Communication and Society*, London 1977.

——, *Reproducing Ideologies*, London 1984.

W.F. Haug, *Critique of Commodity Aesthetics*, London 1985.

J. Donovan, ed, *Feminist Literary Criticism: Explorations in Theory*, Lexington 1975.

Dorothy Hobson, *Crossroads: the Drama of a Soap Opera*, London 1982.

Lee Holcombe, *Victorian Ladies at Work*, Newton Abbot 1973.

——, *Wives and Property*, Oxford 1985.

Patricia Hollis, ed, *Women in Public: the Women's Movement 1850-1900*, London 1979.

Bell Hooks, *Ain't I a Woman?*, London 1981.

Coral Ann Howells, *Love, Mystery and Misery: Feeling in Gothic Fiction*, London 1978.

Derek Hudson, *Munby, Man of Two Worlds*, London 1972.

Rosemary Jackson, *Fantasy: the Literature of Subversion*, London and New York 1981.

Mary Jacobus, ed, *Women Writing and Writing about Women*, London 1979.

Louis James, *Fiction for the Working Men, 1830-1850*, Oxford 1963.

Frederic Jameson, *Marxism and Form*, New York 1971.

——, *The Prison-house of Language*, New York 1972.

——, *The Political Unconscious*, London 1981.

——, 'Postmodernism, or the Cultural Logic of Late Capitalism', *New Left Review*, 146, 1984.

Richard Johnson, 'Barrington Moore, Perry Anderson and English Social Development', in Stuart Hall, et al., eds, *Culture, Media, Language*, London 1980.

Josephine Kamm, *Hope Deferred: Girls' Education in English History*, London 1965.

Cora Kaplan, *Sea Changes: Culture and Feminism*, London 1986.

Elaine Kaye, *A History of Queen's College London*, London 1972.

Gary Kelly, *The English Jacobin Novel, 1780-1805*, Oxford 1976.

Frank Kermode, 'The Buyers Market', *New York Review of Books*, Oct 31, 1974.

Gillian Kersley, *Darling Madame: Sarah Grand and Devoted Friend*, London 1983.

Arnold Kettle, *An Introduction to the English Novel*, London 1951.
Margaret Kirkham, *Jane Austen, Feminism and Fiction*, London 1983.
Annette Kuhn & AnnMarie Wolpe, eds, *Feminism and Materialism: Women and Modes of Production*, London 1978.
G. Levine & U.C. Knoepflmacher, eds, *The Endurance of 'Frankenstein': Essays on Mary Shelley's Novel*, Berkeley 1979.
Jack Lindsay, *George Meredith*, London 1956.
Terry Lovell, *Pictures of Reality*, London 1980.
——, 'Writing Like a Woman: a Question of Politics', in F. Baker et al, eds, *The Politics of Theory*, Colchester 1983.
G. Lukacs, *Writer and Critic*, London 1970.
Colin MacCabe, 'Realism and the Cinema', *Screen*, Vol. 15, 2, 1974.
——, *James Joyce and the Revolution of the Word*, London 1978.
Pierre Machery, *A Theory of Literary Production*, London 1978.
Ellen Malos, ed, *The Politics of Housework*, London 1980.
H. Marcuse, *One-Dimensional Man*, London 1964.
Margaret Mathieson, *The Preachers of Culture*, London 1975.
Robert D. Mayo, *The English Novel in the Magazines, 1740-1815*, Evanston 1962.
Juliet Mitchell, *Women: the Longest Revolution*, London 1984.
Tania Modleski, *Loving with a Vengeance*, London 1982.
Ellen Moers, *Literary Women*, New York 1976.
Toril Moi, *Sexual/Textual Politics*, London 1985.
Franco Moretti, *Signs Taken for Wonders*, London 1983.
Francis Mulhern, *The Moment of Scrutiny*, London 1979.
Janet Murray, ed, *Strong-Minded Women*, Harmondsworth 1984.
Robin Myers & Michael Harris, eds, *Development of the English Book Trade, 1700-1899*, Oxford 1981.
Tom Nairn, 'The English Literary Intelligentsia', *Bananas*, 3, 1976.
——, *The Break-Up of Britain*, London 1977.
J.L. Newton, M.P. Ryan & J.R. Walkowitz, eds, *Sex and Class in Women's History*, London 1983.
D.J. Palmer, *The Rise of English Studies*, London, New York & Toronto 1965.
Chris Pawling, *Popular Fiction and Social Change*, London 1984.
Joyce Senders Pedersen, 'Schoolmistresses and Headmistresses: Elites and Education in Nineteenth Century England', *Journal of British Studies*, 1975.
Anne Phillips, *Divided Loyalties: Dilemmas of Class and Sex*, London 1987.
Ivy Pinchbeck, *Women Workers and the Industrial Revolution, 1750-1850*, London 1981.
Marjorie Plant, *The English Book Trade*, London 1939.
Mary Poovey, *The Proper Lady and the Woman Writer*, Chicago & London 1984.
Mario Praz, *The Romantic Agony*, London 1957.

E. Preteceille & J-P. Terrail, *Capitalism, Consumption and Needs*, Oxford 1985.

David Punter, *The Literature of Terror*, London 1980.

Janice A. Radway, *Reading the Romance*, Chapel Hill & London 1984.

Ruby V. Redinger, *George Eliot: the Emergent Self*, London 1975.

Adrienne Rich, 'Towards a Woman-Centred Unversity', in Rich, *On Lies, Secrets and Silence: Selected Prose, 1966-1978*, London 1980.

Lilian S. Robinson, *Sex, Class and Culture*, New York & London 1978.

K.K. Ruthven, *Feminist Literary Studies: an Introduction*, Cambridge 1984.

Michael Sadleir, *Collecting Yellowbacks*, London 1938.

Lydia Sargeant, ed, *The Unhappy Marriage of Marxism and Feminism*, London 1981.

Janet Sayers, *Biological Politics*, London 1982.

Bernard Sharratt, *Reading Relations: Structures of Literary Production*, London 1985.

Elaine Showalter, *A Literature of Their Own*, London 1979.

Dorothy Smith, 'Women, Class and Family', *Socialist Register*, 1983.

Patricia Meyer Spaacks, *The Female Imagination*, London 1976.

Jane Spencer, *The Rise of the Woman Novelist*, Oxford 1986.

Dale Spender, *Man-Made Language*, London 1980.

——, *Mothers of the Novel*, London 1986.

Michelle Stanworth, *Gender and Schooling*, London 1983.

Carolyn Steedman, *The Tidy House*, London 1982.

——, 'Prisonhouses', *Feminist Review*, 20, 1985.

Lawrence Stone, *The Family, Sex and Marriage in England, 1500-1800*, London 1977.

Ray Strachey, *The Cause*, London 1978.

Patricia Stubbs, *Women and Fiction: Feminism and the Novel, 1880-1920*, London 1979.

Anne Summers, 'A Home from Home — Women's Philanthropic Work in the Nineteenth Century', in S. Burman, ed, *Fit Work for Women*, London 1979.

John Sutherland, *Victorian Novelists and Publishers*, London 1976.

——, *Fiction and the Fiction Industry*, London 1978.

——, *Bestsellers*, London 1981.

Alan Swingewood, *The Myth of Mass Culture*, London 1977.

Barbara Taylor, *Eve and the New Jerusalem*, London 1983.

J.T. Taylor, *Early Opposition to the English Novel, 1760-1830*, New York 1943.

Kathleen Tillotson, *Novels of the Eighteen-Forties*, Oxford 1954.

Tzvetan Todorov, *The Fantastic*, Cornell 1973.

Claire Tomalin, *The Life and Death of Mary Wollstonecraft*, London 1974.

J.M.S. Tompkins, *The Popular Novel in England, 1770-1800*, London 1932.

Margaret J. Tuke, *A History of Bedford College for Women, 1849-1937*, London 1939.

R.P. Utter & G.B. Needham, *Pamela's Daughters*, London 1937.
Judith R. Walkowitz, *Prostitution and Victorian Society*, Cambridge 1980.
——, 'Science, Feminism and Romance: the Men and Women's Club, 1885-1889', *History Workshop Journal*, 21, 1986.
Ian Watt, *The Rise of the Novel*, Harmondsworth 1957.
Arthur Waugh, *One Hundred Years of Publishing*, London 1930.
Igor Webb, *From Custom to Capital: the English Novel and the Industrial Revolution*, New York and London 1981.
Max Weber, *The Protestant Ethic and the Spirit of Capitalism*, London 1930.
Peter Widdowson, ed, *Re-Reading English*, London 1982.
David Williams, *Mr George Eliot: a Biography of George Henry Lewes*, London 1983.
Raymond Williams, *Culture and Society*, London 1960.
——, *The Long Revolution*, London 1961.
——, 'Literature and Sociology: In Memory of Lucien Goldmann', *New Left Review*, 67, 1971.
——, *Television, Technology and Cultural Forms*, London 1973.
——, *Keywords*, London 1976.
——, *Marxism and Literature*, Oxford 1977.
——, *Writing in Society*, London 1983.
Rosalind Williams, *Dream Worlds: Mass Consumption in Late Nineteenth-Century France*, Berkeley, Los Angeles and London 1982.
Janet Wolff, *The Social Production of Art*, London 1981.
——, *Aesthetics and the Sociology of Art*, London 1983.
——, *The Art of Women*, London 1985.
G.M. Young, *Victorian England*, London 1960.
Eli Zaretsky, *Capitalism, the Family and Personal Life*, London 1976.

Index